The
STRENGTHSPATH
Solution

Why Your Career Is Stuck and What To Do About It

A SUCCESSPATH SERIES BOOK

DALE COBB

Published by Career Media, a division of SUCCESSPATH Career Development, Inc.

Career Media books may be purchased in bulk for educational, business, fundraising, or sales promotional use.

Library of Congress Cataloging-in-Publication Data

Cobb, Dale, 1957-
   The STRENGTHSPATH Solution – Why Your Career Is Stuck and What To Do About It/ Dale Cobb

ISBN: 9781798238967

DEDICATION

Thank you to my parents,
Allen and Frances Cobb
who always encouraged me
to pursue my dreams…

And to my beautiful wife and editor
Susy who stood by me when
that wasn't going so well.

CONTENTS

Read This First! I

Prologue   The Morning Sadness V

Section I   Culture

Chapter 1   Deception: Default Paths 1
Chapter 2   Deception: Hot Jobs 5
Chapter 3   Deception: Dead End Jobs 9
Chapter 4   Deception: You Can't Make Money At That 19
Chapter 5   Deception: Degreeism 23
Chapter 6   Deception: Job Description Confusion 29
Chapter 7   Deception: Parental Advice 35
Chapter 8   Deception: You Can't Do Anything 39
Chapter 9   Deception: You Can Do Anything 45
Chapter 10   Deception: Anyone Can Do This 51
Chapter 11   Deception: Change Your Personality 55
Chapter 12   Deception: Deficit Attention Disorder 59
Chapter 13   Deception: Do Whatever It Takes 65
Chapter 14   Deception: Work On Your Weaknesses 69
Chapter 15   Deception: Divisions and Definitions 77
Chapter 16   Deception: False Dichotomy: Work/Play 89

Section II   Circumstances

Chapter 17   Dips – Dead Ends – Dead Horses 95
Chapter 18   Disguises 99
Chapter 19   Dormancy and Delays 105
Chapter 20   Dynamic Tension 111
Chapter 21   Disempowering Forces 117

Section III   The *STRENGTHSPATH* Solution

Chapter 22	Passion	123
Chapter 23	Potential	127
Chapter 24	Personality	137
Chapter 25	Probe	145
Chapter 26	Polish	157
Chapter 27	Package	165
Chapter 28	Promote	171
Chapter 29	Perform	177
Chapter 30	Persevere	183
Chapter 31	Parts	187
Chapter 32	Pace	191
Chapter 33	Prime Time	195
Chapter 34	Plant	199
Chapter 35	Practice	203
Chapter 36	Prune	207
Chapter 37	Partner	211
Chapter 38	Projects	217
Chapter 39	Place	223
Chapter 40	Position	231
Chapter 41	Poppins	235
Chapter 42	Plan	239
Bibliography		242
Coming Titles		250
Resources		251

"There are several different kinds of stuck. Distinguishing one from another is the first step in knowing what to do about it."

~Nick Souter

Read This First!

This isn't a book for other people. This is a book for you! Its purpose is to help you rock career selection... reselection and even resurrection!

Maybe you haven't found your lifework. You could be working in a job that doesn't fit you well. You may even hate your current job. I believe *The STRENGTHSPATH Solution* will be of great help to those of you in the following categories:

Bad Fit - You've found yourself in a job that is clearly a bad fit, but for a variety of reasons, often financial, you need to temporarily suck it up and continue. Most of us find ourselves in this type of situation at least once in our life, sometimes more. In my case, I was raised in a family construction business. At age 13, I began working holidays and summers. For the most part, this was work I just wasn't gifted to excel at. But over time, using some of the ideas in this book, I shaped the work into something tolerable and occasionally enjoyable.

Stepping Stone - You're in a stepping stone job. Your current work is a necessary requirement to move forward. The job is a partial fit but includes several task areas that don't represent your interests or instincts.

Dream Job - You're in your dream job... almost. Most dream jobs require some shaping and molding and carving. Like a great suit of clothes, a good tailor can make it fit perfectly.

It's taken me a long time to zero in on my passion, talent, personality, values and learning style. I spent a lot of time building skills and knowledge in areas that were only loosely connected. I'm writing in hopes that I can help you take a few decades off your career development curve.

This is not a "just think positive book". It's my belief that APTITUDE is just as important as ATTITUDE. It's extremely difficult to go work at something that doesn't match your God-Given abilities every day.

Work on both!!! Work diligently at figuring out your innate design and what type of work fits you best. Most people don't figure this out easily. Tragically, many never do.

I've acquired my knowledge and expertise by studying, experimenting, implementing, reviewing and revising a mass of material from many mentors and role models. These are my insights gathered from hundreds of resources. As you build them around your uniqueness, they should work for you. But let me encourage you to expand on the ideas, create better strategies and then let me know so that I can keep getting better as well.

The book is written in a sequence with concepts that are designed to build on each other. But feel free to skip around and cherry-pick ideas and start putting the information into action quickly.

You may be a person who would do much better in a completely different role. To help you find that role, I recommend my other book, *The STRENGTHSPATH Principle*. In the meantime, give these ideas a try.

The STRENGTHSPATH Solution is not a book that encourages rebellion or anarchy. Lines of authority are critical for a well-functioning organization. Some of the ideas can't be implemented in every single situation. You shouldn't even try to begin shaping your job in the first month. In most structured environments, you'll need to begin following instructions. Over time, you can ask for permission and buy-in. Sometimes you'll have to negotiate changes. Implementing these ideas will require wisdom, judgment and timing.

I worked 16 years in a corporate environment. In the first few months I did everything as I was told. Their system was outstanding and their training was phenomenal. Over time I adjusted the job to fit my unique abilities.

The STRENGTHSPATH Solution is not a book that encourages a dysfunctional work ethic. I love what Peter Buffett has to say on this topic in *Life Is What You Make It*. Buffett writes, "Some people believe that having a good work ethic equates with a willingness to slave away for sixty or eighty hours a week, at a job for which one has no passion for or even actively hates. The idea here is that the sheer effort, self-denial, and time logged on the clock are somehow intrinsically virtuous."

Buffet continues, "That's not virtue; it's masochism! In some cases it's also, paradoxically, a sign of laziness and lack of imagination. If you're such a hard worker, why not use some of that effort and some of those hours to find something you actually like? The essence of a good work ethic starts with meeting a challenge of self-discovery, finding something you love to do, so that work – even, or especially, when it is difficult and arduous – becomes joyful, maybe even sacred."

Most of your job should be enjoyable. If it's not, you're either doing it wrong, have failed to shape it or you're in a job you are not cut out for.

The STRENGTHSPATH Solution is divided into three sections. The first section is on cultural barriers. What are the popular concepts within the culture that cause you to make bad career decisions? The second section is on poor personal choices. What decisions have you made that are resulting in negative consequences? The third section is loaded with specific strategies and solutions. Most readers will be able to put a few of the strategies to work the next day. Some methods may need to wait until you have more experience or are in a job that allows more flexibility.

"Our natural human tendency is to think of ourselves as independent and authentic - authors of our own destinies. But that's a tall order and much tougher than it seems. Bombarded by external triggers and expectations, we can easily fall into roles and patterns established for us by other people."

~Alan Weiss, from *Lifestorming*

PROLOGUE
The Morning Sadness

Have you felt "**The Morning Sadness**"?

M. Night Shyamalan's film, *Unbreakable,* with Bruce Willis and Samuel Jackson is a bit dark, but it has one scene that is priceless.

The movie's lead character, David (Bruce Willis), is working as a security guard. After surviving a train wreck without a scratch, he discovers he actually has the powers of a superhero.

Here is a brief dialogue from an early scene in the film:

David (Bruce Willis), *"This morning was the first morning I can remember, that I didn't open my eyes and feel that sadness."*

Elijah (Samuel Jackson), *"That little bit of sadness in the mornings you spoke of? I think I know what that is. **Perhaps you're not doing what you're supposed to be doing.**"*

According to statistics from a wide variety of sources, many of us are feeling that same sadness. The vast majority are not working powerfully, purposefully or passionately. Most workers realize very little of their potential, don't experience much peace or satisfaction, and their paycheck remains a fraction of what it could be.

Richard Chang writes, "We spend a lot of time doing things we don't want to do in places we don't want to be for no other reason than we feel we have to. We have to bring home a paycheck, please our friends and family, and meet the expectations the world has set for us. If nothing else, we find ourselves in less than ideal situations out of habit. We follow the path our lives begin to take and are too afraid, or reluctant, to change our course as time goes by."

Stanford University Life Design Instructors Bill Burnett & Dave Evans report, "In America, two-thirds of workers are unhappy with their jobs. And 15 percent actually hate their work. In the United States alone, more than thirty-one million people between the ages of forty-four and seventy want what is called an encore career – work that combines personal meaning, continued income, and social impact."

According to *Deloitte Consulting*, 65% of U.S. workers are planning to leave their current employer.

A *Harris Interactive* poll of 7,718 workers said:
42% of workers feel burnt out
33% feel dead ended (They see no future in their job.)
85% do not feel strongly energized by their work

Franklin Covey polled 23,000 workers finding that:
80% of employees feel unenthusiastic about their goals
50% feel dissatisfied with their work at the end of the week

Gallup has polled several million workers revealing:
20% or less of us get to "do what we do best" on a daily basis

The *U.S. Bureau of Labor Statistics* reports:
67% of Americans don't like their jobs

Think of the negative impact that has on an organization! But also think about the negative impact on individuals and their families.

Indeed released a comprehensive study of 8,000 adults. The analysis

VI

revealed that nearly two in three workers look for another job within the first three months of starting a new one.

And a survey of more than 3,000 workers by *CareerBuilder* found that roughly one in three workers say they are regularly looking for a new job — no matter what job they currently have.

Nicholas Lore, author of *The Pathfinder,* also co-authored another book, *What Now,* with Anthony Spadafore. Both Nick and Anthony are two of America's top career designers. Nick has received accommodations for his work from two U.S. Presidents for helping over 14,000 individuals make career transitions. Nick and Anthony offer estimates that line up closely with the survey statistics I just sited. Their data shows:

10% of Americans see their work as passionate play
20% see their work as a positive most of the time
30% are neutral
30% are negative to the point of causing dysfunction or disruption
10% are actually in career hell (They may be dangerous)

Our language frequently betrays our underlying feelings about our work. We talk about...
"Monday Morning Blues" (this often begins on Sunday evening)
Needing a **"Mental Health Day"**
Wednesday is **"Hump Day"** when we can begin looking forward to the weekend
"Happy Hour" begins when we get off work and ingest the numbing agent of choice
"Thank God it's Friday - TGIF"
We go **"Back to the grind"**
"I can't wait for retirement"
"I'm just going through the paces"
"Tell me again why I'm here"
"I just never seem to get ahead"
"It's not my dream job, but it's only for a year"
"I hate my job, but so does everyone"

"I'm stuck in a dead-end job"

I have three-plus decades of workplace experience including a decade as an entrepreneur, a decade as a sales representative and over a decade as manager, trainer and career development professional. All of my experience validates the workplace language and sited numbers. Most people are massively unhappy with their work.

Autobiography In Five Short Chapters
By Portia Nelson

Chapter 1: I walk down the street. There is a deep hole in the sidewalk. I fall in. I am lost… I am helpless. It isn't my fault. It takes me forever to find my way out.

Chapter 2: I walk down the same street. There is a deep hole in the sidewalk. I pretend I don't see it. I fall in again. I can't believe I am in the same place, but it isn't my fault. It still takes me a long time to get out.

Chapter 3: I walk down the same street. There is a deep hole in the sidewalk. I see it is still there. I still fall in. It's a habit. My eyes are open. I know where I am. It is my fault. I get out immediately.

Chapter 4: I walk down the same street. There is a deep hole in the sidewalk. I walk around it.

Chapter 5: I walk down another street.

How long does it take you to change a pattern that isn't working? Most of us need to find some new sidewalks at work. A lot of success in life comes from knowing what we want to avoid. Warren Buffett's business partner Charlie Munger often says, "Tell me where I'm going to die so I'll never go there." Munger continues, "It's remarkable how much long-term advantage we have gotten by trying to be consistently not stupid, instead of trying to be very intelligent."

This book is designed to help you identify the deep career holes that most people fall into and then get on another sidewalk quickly!

Section I
The Culture Problem

In this first section we'll look at career selection problems that are largely cultural. Finding yourself in the wrong career is not all your fault. But it is your responsibility to identify the thinking and forces that got you where you are and to move in more positive directions. If you find yourself in a hole, rule #1 is to stop digging. Rule #2 is to understand a bit about the hole and the pathways that led you there. Rule #3 is to find your way out of the hole!

"Just follow the yellow brick road."

~Glinda, Good Witch of the North

CHAPTER 1
Deception: Default Paths

The Lemming Conspiracy is a concept written about in Bob McDonald and Don E. Hutcheson's book, *Don't Waste Your Talent.* In legend, these small arctic animals band together in vast herds. Running in groups, they sometimes head for a cliff and run to their deaths. Their commitment to the herd kills them.

Zig Ziglar in his classic, *See You At The Top*, tells a similar story about processionary caterpillars. Apparently you can line them up in a circle to follow each other, set their favorite food in the middle of the circle and they will starve to death. Like the Lemmings, their commitment to following kills them.

In his blog, Seth Godin writes about getting our default settings right, "We know that the defaults determine the behavior of the group. Organ donation, 401k allocations, the typeface on our word processor - the way it's set to act if we don't override it is often the way we act. Because often, we decide it's not worth the effort to change the setting today. Which means that examining your settings now and then is worth the effort:

Don't speak unless asked vs. don't keep quiet with a suggestion.

Look for the downsides vs. look for the upsides.

Do the minimum vs. do the maximum.

Don't ship until perfect vs. ship and learn.

The benefit of the doubt vs. skepticism.

Trusting vs. wary.

Inquiry vs. sarcasm.

Speed up vs. slow down.

Generous vs. selfish.

We all have defaults. Are yours helping you?"

Each of us is on some kind of a track. Most of us are either blind to the track (we don't see it), or we never question it. This path is often a set of expectations. In most cases those expectations come from our culture including parents, peers, professors, pastors and partners. There is a whole new set of forces that try to shape us once we enter our first job and then our profession.

The American Dream is one of those default pathways and it comes in many expressions. There is the white picket fence home ownership American Dream, the six-figure income American Dream, the 2.5 children American Dream, the corner office American Dream and so on.

In his book *The Dream Chaser*, Tony Gaskins writes, "We all have a path set in place from the moment we're born. The problem is we don't usually question that path. We just hop on and follow it and allow it to lead us to misery. Sometimes we reach the destination and then finally get the guts to get off the birth path and go in a new direction. Right now there are artists who can change the world with their art, but they've settled for being a lawyer in their small city, handling routine cases. Right now, there are philanthropists who can help relieve hunger in thousands of lives, but they've settled for being an accountant because they were told that was a great major in college."

Gaskins continues, "You have to question the path. We all need to write our own road map that will lead us to where we want to be, not where we are told we should be. Are you extremely happy doing what you're doing for a living? If not, you're on the wrong path. Don't follow a path to misery. The wrong path is handed down from generation to generation. The American Dream became a nightmare for many because they didn't realize that the dream they were pursuing wasn't their dream. It was the dream someone else had created for them."

Think about your current career path. How did you get on that path? Did you choose your path based on a clear understanding of your passionate interests, talents and values? If not, you're probably on the wrong path.

"Forget about the hot jobs... Get in touch with what burns inside you."

~Dale Cobb

CHAPTER 2
Deception: Hot Jobs

There are many lists of "Hot Jobs" or "In-Demand Careers" circulating in newspapers, magazines, books, career service offices, admissions offices and on internet websites. The authors of these lists claim to have the inside track on which jobs are growing in number and therefore worth training for. Here is one such list:

Career possibility #1:   Personal/Home Health Aide
Career possibility #2:   Medical Assistant
Career possibility #3:   Mental Health Counselor/Social Worker
Career possibility #4:   Network Systems and Communications Analyst
Career possibility #5:   Computer Software Applications Engineer
Career possibility #6:   Teacher
Career possibility #7:   Paralegal/Legal Assistant
Career possibility #8:   Financial Services
Career possibility #9:   Accountant and Auditor
Career possibility #10: Employment Services

The problems with using this type of list for career selection and direction are many, but let me share a few:

First, job growth and shrinkage is a very dynamic, even volatile thing. It's not much different than the stock market.

Second, following the educational career path suggested to reach some of these jobs, may take longer than the growth curve period. The career opportunity may no longer be in demand once you complete school. In fact, if enough people follow this strategy, and many do, that career may actually be over supplied with applicants once you are job ready.

Third, supply and demand is very local. Most job trend statistics are based on national averages and may have nothing to do with your local economy and job market. I've coached many clients who live in rural areas with almost no job opportunities that match their training.

Fourth, these figures are tossed around very loosely and are not regulated. No one is held accountable for the accuracy. In some cases, corporations wishing to reduce labor costs may falsely report a need for workers so that they can create a surplus pool of employees.

Fifth, the numbers are often used by recruiters (salespeople) who have a profit motive. There is nothing wrong with that if the numbers are accurate. But always remember Warren Buffett's advice, "Don't ask a barber if you need a haircut."

Sixth, the demand of the job shouldn't be your primary criteria for deciding which career to pursue. I want to say, job growth or demand shouldn't be any part of the criteria, but I don't quite believe that. But it should be a relatively minor part. **Criteria #1 should be passion for the work and enjoyment of the daily tasks**.

Seventh, the **#2 criteria should be underlying natural talent for the work and the daily tasks**. I've said it many times, shoeing horses hasn't been an in-demand career for over a century. But there are still people making a living putting shoes on horses. If you love horses and have the aptitudes for the work, this is a much better option than the latest hot job or in-demand career choice. Of course there should be a marketplace need, but it doesn't have to be huge or even growing rapidly.

If you want to look at the job numbers, fine. Trust and verify. Look for current job postings in your area. Track them for at least a month or two. Consider the different schools in your area who are graduating students with skills in that profession. Set up an informational interview with at least three people responsible to hire those positions when they come open. Get their input on demand. See if you can set up a job shadow. Get a sense if this is something you would be good at and enjoy doing.

"The society which scorns excellence in plumbing as a humble activity and tolerates shoddiness in philosophy because it is an exalted activity will have neither good plumbing nor good philosophy: neither its pipes nor its theories will hold water."

~John W. Gardner

CHAPTER 3
Deception: Dead End Jobs

There are no dead end jobs, only dead end mindsets. The "Dead End Job Deception" is pervasive in today's American culture and it comes in at least 4 versions. We believe that certain jobs have no future. But as cultural architect, Erwin McManus states, "Your future is within you."

I believe there are people wandering around disconnected from their unique destiny because they have bought into this deception. Many are hoping to do something important with their life, like play basketball or become a rocket scientist, all the while their true genius is in fast food operations, retail or somehow working with their hands. They could have been working at the C-Suite level at *In-n-Out* if they had just been willing to start flipping burgers. They could have been working at the C-Suite level at *Nordstrom* had they just been willing to fold and stock clothes. They could have owned their own *Harley-Davidson* dealership had they just been willing to get their hands greasy on a motorcycle chain. Or they could have set up a very successful farming operation had they believed it was worth starting in the fields. Let's look at some people who were willing.

Version 1: The Fast-Food Dead End Job

Probably no job is more maligned than working at a fast food restaurant. Most of us assume this job is beneath us and in many cases beneath our kids. I interviewed *McDonald's* franchise owner, Art Bender when I was in my early twenties. The takeaway from the interview was that successful franchise owners were more than willing to clean the restrooms and do other "dirty" jobs. Nothing was beneath them. I keep in my files a story I ran across in1996. The article described the career of Susan Steele who began her climb up the corporate ladder repeating one great question day after day, "**Do you want fries with that?**"

The first stop on Susan's climb was a job at a *McDonald's* fast-food restaurant in Phoenix in 1972. Step-by-step she moved up the rungs to vice-president in charge of the chain's Bay Area region. She sat in her headquarters office in north San Jose, responsible for 500 corporate-owned *McDonald's* outlets and 5,000 employees. Her question, "Why all the put-downs of fast-food jobs? We resent it when people say, 'You don't want to end up flipping hamburgers all your life.'"

Steel started out, after graduating early from high school, making milk shakes, and from there moved to the front counter. She gently pushed to work the grill, which in those days, was a male dominated job. She enjoyed it so much she changed her plans to pursue literature in college and put her initial career goal of teaching school on hold.

By age 19, she was newly married and supervising workers. She bootstrapped her way to swing manager and then moved into the salaried assistant manager ranks. "I made the decision not to continue community college when I was promoted to assistant manager. I was thinking, I really like this. I'm going to do this for a while." Five years after she mixed her first milk shake she was given her own restaurant to manage. Successful there, she was then asked to open a new *McDonald's*. She was promoted to field supervisor overseeing relations with owner-operated restaurants in the region and then went to Chicago to teach classes at *Hamburger University*.

Then came a move to San Diego working as director of operations and then the move to San Jose overseeing the entire Bay Area. At that juncture she had become an officer of the company. Steele said, "I finally made that, in the time frame I'd set for myself. All the way along I had precise

10

goals. I wanted to be at a certain place by a certain date, and I wanted to be very good at it when I got there, not just have a title."

Can you say "McOpportunity"? There are no dead end jobs… only dead end approaches and dead end attitudes! Today, 20 years later, the opportunities are even better. *In-n-Out Burger, Chipotle* and *Starbucks* to name a few, are now on the scene and looking for people that want a career.

Version 2: The Retail Clerk Dead End Job

Close behind flipping burgers would be the almost equally maligned "retail store clerk". Marcus Buckingham shares the inspiring story of Tami Heim in his fantastic book, *The One Thing You Need to Know.*

Tami always had a fascination with stores. So great was her fascination that by the age of twelve, she knew she wanted to go into retail. Actually, that's not entirely true. She started playing store with her friends much earlier than that. But it was only as she reached age twelve that she started talking about it seriously.

She was urged by her uncle, at age sixteen, to test out her fascination by applying at a local department store. She applied at *Lazarus* in her hometown of Indianapolis. She was told they weren't hiring any part-timers, but because she was unclear what part-time meant she sat in the waiting room all day in hopes she would get hired. She was finally granted an interview with the operations manager and her passion won him over.

At first, managers delegated all the tough jobs to show her that real life retail wasn't all fun and games. But Tami says she was addicted from the beginning. She loved the immediate feedback of retail, where you can quickly see the impact of a display change. She loved the theatre of it and the everyday drama of putting on a show for thousands of customers. As she put it, "I just couldn't imagine anything more exciting than coming in everyday and having a chance to do that."

She worked at the store all the way through high school and through her years studying retail management at *Purdue University*. After graduation she was placed in a management training program and steadily moved up through the ranks from department manager, to manager of a small store, then manager of a larger store. There were setbacks along the way. Her parent company went into bankruptcy, but she maintained her passion.

Then one day *Borders* called. She was first hired as one of their territorial vice-presidents responsible for the western U.S. Only two years later, she was asked to assume the role of company president. During her tenure, profits shot up and the stock price grew 66%.

Let's establish once and for all, **the only dead end job is the one you are not talented for and passionate about**.

Patrick McCarthy arrived at a then small regional seven-store retail chain in 1971 at the age of 26. He had found his former job as a prison counselor frustrating and mentally draining. Patrick was looking for something where he might have more talent.

Unfortunately, he was ill prepared for the job, and as he says, "I made every mistake in the book." As a beginner in the men's department he knew nothing about clothes or personal style. He wore his shirts too big, he didn't know how to fold garments for display, and knew nothing of how to coordinate color and texture. Worse...after working at *Nordstrom* for less than two years, he had developed a reputation for being uncooperative, hard to manage, and a poor team player.

But then things began to shift. He found a mentor by the name of Ray Black. Also a *Nordstrom* manager, Patrick Kennedy, took McCarthy under his wing and began to develop him. McCarthy says, during his 7th year his business started to take off. At one point his client list included 40 lawyers from one firm alone.

After 30 years, Patrick McCarthy retired in 2001 as *Nordstrom's* All-Time Top Salesman. In fact… for 15 consecutive years, he was the number one salesperson throughout the entire chain. If you feel a tug toward retail, I can think of no better introduction than a book he co-wrote with Robert Spector titled *The Nordstrom Way*.

Version 3: The Work With Your Hands Dead End Job

I never worked in fast food or as a clerk in retail but I spent many years working with my hands. I did this first in my dad's construction business, then in my own small plaster/stucco business, and finally as a wall-covering contractor. The last gig went on for almost 10 years until I reached my early 30s. During this time, I was surrounded with talent, some of it world class, and I sought them out as mentors and coaches. One of them was Larry Spitler, an insanely great wall covering installer who traveled all over the country putting together teams that did installations on huge Las Vegas Hotels, commercial buildings, and high-end homes. Larry helped me install a 300 dollar per roll hand screened silk from Thailand.

At the end of the day, I didn't inherit the mechanical aptitude to match the environment I was planted in, even though it was rich with opportunity. I left working with my hands in 1991 and never looked back. I learned there is abundant opportunity to build a lucrative career working with your hands if you have the aptitude and passion for it. But the opportunity is never enough. I also learned, there is a considerable bias in this culture against working with your hands, regardless of the opportunity it offers to those so wired. I could feel this bias almost every time I made a banking transaction in my stellar white wall-covering uniform. The days I banked in nice casual clothing or even a suit brought much better treatment from the tellers. Matthew Crawford digs into this bias deeply, first in an article he wrote for *New York Times Magazine* and then in the book *Shop Class as Soul Craft.* Crawford writes:

"High-school shop-class programs were widely dismantled in the 1990s as educators prepared students to become 'knowledge workers'. The imperative of the last 20 years to round up every warm body and send it to college, then to the cubicle, was tied to a vision of the future in which we somehow take leave of material reality and glide about in a pure information economy. This has not come to pass. To begin with, such work often feels more enervating than gliding. More fundamentally, now as ever,

13

somebody has to actually do things: fix our cars, unclog our toilets, build our houses."

Crawford continues, "When we praise people who do work that is straight forwardly useful, the praise often betrays an assumption that they had no other options. We idealize them as the salt of the earth and emphasize the sacrifice for others their work may entail. Such sacrifice does indeed occur — the hazards faced by a lineman restoring power during a storm come to mind.

This seems to be a moment when the useful arts have an especially compelling economic rationale. A car mechanics' trade association reports that repair shops have seen their business jump significantly in the current recession: people aren't buying new cars; they are fixing the ones they have. The current downturn is likely to pass eventually. But there are also systemic changes in the economy, arising from information technology, that have the surprising effect of making the manual trades — plumbing, electrical work, car repair — more attractive as careers. The *Princeton* economist Alan Blinder argues that the crucial distinction in the emerging labor market is not between those with more or less education, but between those whose services can be delivered over a wire and those who must do their work in person or on site. The latter will find their livelihoods more secure against outsourcing to distant countries. As Blinder puts it, 'You can't hammer a nail over the Internet.' Nor can the Indians fix your car, because they are in India.

If the goal is to earn a living, then, maybe it isn't really true that 18-year-olds need to be imparted with a sense of panic about getting into college (though they certainly need to learn). Some people are hustled off to college, then to the cubicle, against their own inclinations and natural bents, when they would rather be learning to build things or fix things. One shop teacher suggested to me that 'in schools, we create artificial learning environments for our children that they know to be contrived and undeserving of their full attention and engagement. Without the opportunity to learn through the hands, the world remains abstract and distant, and the passions for learning will not be engaged.'"

Crawford concludes, "A gifted young person who chooses to become a mechanic rather than to accumulate academic credentials is viewed as eccentric, if not self-destructive. There is a pervasive anxiety among parents that there is only one track to success for their children. It runs through a series of gates controlled by prestigious institutions. Further, there is wide use of drugs to medicate boys, especially, against their natural tendency toward action, the better to 'keep things on track.' I taught briefly in a public high school and would have loved to have set up a *Ritalin* fogger in my classroom. It is a rare person, male or female, who is naturally inclined to sit still for 17 years in school, and then indefinitely at work.

The trades suffer from low prestige, and I believe this is based on a simple mistake. Because the work is dirty, many people assume it is also stupid. This is not my experience. I have a small business as a motorcycle mechanic in Richmond, Va., which I started in 2002. I work on Japanese and European motorcycles, mostly older bikes with some 'vintage' cachet that makes people willing to spend money on them. I have found the satisfactions of the work to be very much bound up with the intellectual challenges it presents. And yet my decision to go into this line of work is a choice that seems to perplex many people."

Version 4: The Agriculture Dead End Job

I live in an agricultural area. When you think about California, many things probably come to mind. Sunny and 77. The beaches. The crazies. Hollywood. But I live in the heart of California where farming and ranching is king.

In Visalia, California where I lived for a decade, there was a saying **"Smells Like Money"**. A dairy was on every corner. No matter what part of town you lived in, whether you were upwind or downwind, it was going to

15

smell like money. If you haven't figured it out yet, I'm referring to the manure odor that always accompanies dairy farming.

My grandfather moved to Central California in the 1920s. He came to work as a farm laborer. They lived in tents. Today they would have been considered homeless. But my grandfather had a dream and honestly, he was a bit of a genius. His job was tending a fairly young walnut orchard. He went to his employer and asked if he could plant cotton in between the rows of trees and work it on his time off. His employer agreed and that's how he got his start in farming. My grandfather loved farming and I still have memories of traveling around with him in his pick up truck setting water and checking the cotton. To this day, seeing really healthy cotton gives me a positive emotional charge.

He took that seed money profit and bought some land. Then he bought some more land. His dream was to have one piece of property to leave to each of his kids, which he accomplished before he passed away. He also had phenomenal mechanical aptitudes. He was an inventor who invented farm equipment and had several patents to his name.

Nice story... What's my point? Today, like retail, like fast food, like working with your hands, agriculture is often looked down upon as a way to make a living. The opportunities are still there. But many overlook the opportunities because all they see is a dead end job.

I received an email recently from Michael Senoff. Actually, Michael is a marketing genius and I get an email from him regularly. But that's a different story for a different day. Michael sent me an attachment with his email that told a story about a man who grew up on a fruit tree farm. As a teenager he was set up with a little fruit stand to make some extra money. He had a knack for it, and just kept trying out new ways to improve sales. He experimented with location, signage, everything. Over time he came up with a very successful system. Then, he started hiring people to man the stands and multiplied the whole operation.

You and I are blind to 100s of opportunities to make a lot of money. We could be working with our talents. But we don't. The job is hidden behind a type of work that we have been taught has no potential. How many times have you and I both driven by a fruit stand imagining that the owner was struggling to get by?

Don't rush out and start a fruit stand. Don't go out and buy a cow. Just don't overlook the opportunity that you are drawn toward because you are "sure" you couldn't make a living doing that kind of work. And maybe even more important, don't discourage your kids from pursuing something that they are drawn to because you can't imagine a good income. And that leads us to the next "Deception"....

"There are no menial jobs, just menial attitudes."

~Justice William J. Brennan

CHAPTER 4
Deception: You Can't Make Money At That...

One of my favorite organizations is *ROADTRIP NATION*. They believe, "If you can dream it up, somebody is probably getting a paycheck for it." The organization hosts a lot of school assemblies encouraging students to begin thinking about their dream jobs. They routinely ask for dream job ideas from the crowd, a dangerous idea when working with middle and high school kids. In their latest book, *ROADMAP*, they tell the story of an assembly student who claimed he wanted to become a "turtle walker". Within minutes the *Roadtrip Nation* team went to *Google*, found the position and made a call to the *Hidden Harbor Marine Environmental Project* in Florida. Before he knew what happened, the young man was speaking to a real life turtle walker on the phone.

Both *The Millionaire Next Door,* by Thomas J. Stanley and William D. Danko and the follow-up book, *The Millionaire Mind,* penned only by Stanley, were well-researched, well-documented material on the backgrounds and behaviors of the wealthy in the United States. They both had a number of good useable principles and clearly communicated that most wealth is generated by great work as opposed to good investments.

But two points jumped off the pages at me. In *The Millionaire Mind,* Stanley did the homework on how millionaires in this country selected their careers and line of work. Overwhelmingly, when given all kinds of options, they said **they chose based on aptitude. In other words their own understanding of their individual strengths drove their decision far more than any other factor.**

The second point, was the sheer number of different types of businesses the self-employed millionaires came from. **Our culture would have us believe that only a few kinds of work really offer an opportunity for economic success.** Look at the different kinds of businesses that produced millionaire status. The list below is alphabetical and shows only the jobs starting with A thru K. The full list is much longer.

Accountant, Accounting/Auditing Services, Advertising Agency, Advertising Specialty Distributor, Advertising/Marketing Advisor, Aerospace Consultant, Agriculture, Ambulance Service, Antique Sales, Apartment Complex Owner/Manager, Apparel Manufacturer-Sportswear, Apparel Manufacturer-Infant Wear, Apparel Manufacturer-Ready To Wear, Apparel Retailer-Wholesaler-Ladies Fashions, Artist Commercial, Attorney, Attorney-Entertainment Industry, Attorney-Real Estate, Auctioneer, Auctioneer-Appraiser, Audio/Video Reproduction, Author-Fiction, Author-Text Books/Training Manuals, Automotive Leasing, Baked Goods Producer, Beauty Salon(s) Owner Manager, Beer Wholesaler, Beverage Machinery Manufacturer, Bovine Semen Distributor, Brokerage/Sales, Builder, Builder/Real Estate Developer, Business/Real Estate Broker/Investor, Cafeteria Owner, Candy/Tobacco Wholesaler, Caps/Hats Manufacturer, Carpet Manufacturer, Citrus Fruits Farmer, Civil Engineer and Surveyor, Clergyman-Lecturer, Clinical Psychologist, Coin and Stamp Dealer, Commercial Laundry, Commercial Real Estate Management, Commercial Laboratory, Commercial Property Management, Commodity Brokerage Company, Computer Consultant, Computer Applications Consultant, Construction, Construction Equipment Dealer, Construction Equipment Manufacturing, Construction-Mechanical/Electrical, Construction Performance Insurance, Consultant, Consulting Geologist, Contract Feeding, Contractor, Convenience Food Stores Owner, Cotton Gin Operator, Cotton Farmer, Cotton Ginning Owner/Manager, CPA/Broker, CPA/Financial Planner, Curtain Manufacturer, Dairy Farmer, Dairy Products Manufacturer, Data Services, Dentist,

Dentist-Orthodontist, Department Store Owner, Design/Engineering/Builder, Developer/Construction, Diesel Engine Rebuilder/Distributor, Direct Mail Services, Direct Marketing, Direct Marketing Service Organization,Display and Fixture Manufacturer, Donut Maker Machine Manufacturer, Electrical Supply Wholesaler,Employment Agency Owner/Manager, Energy Production Engineer/Consultant, Energy Consultant, Engineer/Architect,Excavation Contractor, Excavation/Foundation Contracting, Executive Transportation/Bodyguard Service, Farmer,Fast Food Restaurants, Financial Consultant, Florist Retailer/Wholesaler, Freight Agent, Fruit and Vegetable Distributor,Fuel Oil Dealer, Fuel Oil Distributor, Fund Raiser/Consultant, Funeral Home Operator, Furniture Manufacturing,General Agent Insurance Agency, General Contractor, Grading Contractor, Grocery Wholesaler, Grocery Store Retailer,Heat Transfer Equipment Manufacturer, Home Health Care Service, Home Builder/Developer, Home Repair/Painting,Home Furnishings, Horse Breeder, Human Resources Consulting Services, Import-Export, Independent Investment Manager, Independent Insurance Agency, Industrial Laundry/Dry Cleaning Plant, Industrial Chemicals-Cleaning/Sanitation Manufacturer, Information Services, Installations Contractor, Insurance Agent, Insurance Agency Owner, Insurance Adjusters,Investment Management, Irrigated Farm Land Realtor-Lessee, Janitorial Services Contractor,Janitorial Supply-Wholesaler Distributor, Janitorial Contractor, Jewelry Retailer/Wholesaler,Job Training/Vocational Tech School Owner, Koolin Mining-Processing-Sales, Kitchens and Bath Distributor.

Next time your son or daughter comes and tells you they want to go into some line of work that makes you raise your eyebrow a bit... say, "Bring it on!!!!" The next time a friend or family member pours water on your dream, remember the turtle walker.

"Employees without any college education are just as (if not more) valuable as those with a traditional degree. After two or three years, your ability to perform… is completely unrelated to how you performed when you were in school. The skills you required in college are very different. You're also fundamentally a different person. You learn and grow, you think about things differently."

~Lazlo Block, *Google*, Director of People Operations

CHAPTER 5
Deception: Degreeism

I'm going to start with what I consider to be a wise quote from investor Warren Buffet. "Never ask a barber if you need a haircut." Of course the implication is that a barber will always tell you that you need a haircut because they have a vested financial interest in the answer. I recently had a coaching session with a college recruiter. One thing that came out during that session was the amount of pressure he was under to meet a quota of students enrolled in a graduate program. This guy was an honest hard worker who I'm confident placed his potential students above his university's need to keep enrollment up. But make sure you keep Warren Buffet's comment in mind when you decide to purchase an education.

Let me cut to the chase. There is a deception about the need for college degrees today. Snobbery exists in a few educational circles. We see it in many forms. Some consistently suggest that you can't succeed or be a productive member of society without jumping through their sometimes ridiculous ceremonious hoops.

If you are a teacher or a student don't misunderstand what I'm saying here. I believe a good education is critical in establishing the foundation for success. I'm just suggesting that some of our institutions aren't as good or as necessary as they think they are in providing this foundation. And in a few cases they actually confound, confuse, and destroy initiative and hope.

If you believe a college degree is a pre-requisite for success, let me drop a few names on you. Each of the following either dropped out or never attended college in the first place:

Successful people include Steve Jobs, Bill Gates, Paul Allen, Richard Branson, Lawrence Ellison, Kirk Kerkorian, David Geffen, John Richard Simplot, Theodore W. Waitt, Wayne Huizenga, Ralph Lauren, Joseph Albertson, Michael Dell, Coco Chanel, Tony Robbins, Eric Hoffer, Andy Rooney, Barry Diller, Thomas Edison and Walt Disney.

Nine U.S. Presidents didn't have degrees including Harry Truman, Abraham Lincoln, Andrew Jackson, Andrew Johnson, George Washington, Grover Cleveland, Martin Van Buren, Millard Fillmore and Zachary Taylor. Eleanor Roosevelt, arguably one of the most effective first ladies, never attended college.

Entertainment professionals without a degree include Leonardo DiCaprio, Tracy Morgan, Stephen Spielberg, Kate Winslet, Harrison Ford, Frank Sinatra, Sean Connery, Michael J. Fox, Simon Cowell, Rachel Ray, Eddie Murphy, Sarah Michelle Gellar, Jon Bon Jovi, Avril Lavigne, Steve Martin, Charleton Heston and Elvis Presley.

In the 1980's I read a study reported by a seminary professor. He shared that of the lead pastors in the 100 largest churches in America, 75 did not have seminary degrees.

Journalists include Walter Cronkite, Peter Jennings and Larry King.

Scientists include Buckminster Fuller and Erik Erickson.

Artist types include Frank Lloyd Wright and Earnest Hemmingway and William Faulkner.

Many of them became billionaires. All of them have been off the charts successful. And this is only a partial list of some of the more famous names. I have quite a file going on these people. I could go on by telling you about the *University of Chicago* study reporting that those with college degrees have less sex and that those with postgraduate degrees have the least sex of all. I could tell you about the $500,000 you would have in the bank at age 50 if you took your $120,000 college education fund and invested it in a meager municipal bond paying only 5%. I could tell you

24

about the fuzzy math, educational "salespeople" use to convince you that your earnings will be higher if you get a college degree. But I won't...

Again, I'm not saying don't go to college or don't get a degree. In many cases college is a very useful step. In some cases like medicine, it is a necessary step. College can also be a great place to explore and discover your passion. Use school and college as one tool in your bag on the road to a good education built around your unique talents.

By most accounts, inside and outside, our educational system is broken. Forty years ago the United States had the number one educational system in the world. As I write this we stand at nineteenth. Approximately 6,000 kids drop out of high school every day. I have had numerous friends that work as educators. The reports of chaos and fighting are frightening... **and that's just the administrators**. What they have to deal with in the classroom is beyond belief. What should be environments of help and hope toward a better future have become dungeons of discouragement and despair. And this is the environment that is supposed to hold the keys to our children's future.

If you are a passionate educator or gifted teacher, keep fighting the good fight! I know there are thousands of you working hard and long. And the news isn't all bad. There are pockets of greatness springing up all over the country. A teacher here, a charter school there, and even occasionally we see a whole school district excelling. If you haven't taken an education module online from the *Kahn Academy*, put down this book and take one. It has changed the game.

But I want to address two flaws that we rarely hear discussed in any forum on educational reform.

The first flaw is generalized intelligence testing that has often come packaged as the *Stanford-Binet*, now in its 5th version. This instrument is designed to test five areas including fluid reasoning, knowledge, quantitative reasoning, visual-spatial processing, and working memory. The problem is that it still cuts a very narrow swath in terms of possible talents that can be productively applied in ways that could make both a contribution to society and earn substantial income.

As *Harvard* professor Howard Gardner likes to point out, the *Stanford-Binet* and tests like it tend to erroneously ask, "How smart are you?" **instead of the more helpful question, "How are you smart?"** This simple reorganization of four words has enormous implications. The solution, which is already showing up in the more progressive learning institutions is the adoption of "Multiple Intelligence" concepts and methods in the classroom. If you have children of any age, don't wait to develop a working knowledge of these ideas. A good primer for the uninitiated is Thomas Armstrong's *Seven Kinds of Smart.*

The second flaw is Academic Scorecards, specifically the *SAT*, which is a college entrance exam. Educator Jenifer Fox reports:

"Since 1983, *U.S. News and World Report* magazine has ranked *America's 100 Best Colleges.* This publication has changed the way parents and students choose institutions of higher education, leading them to believe that the value of a college degree is only as good as its brand name. For the past 25 years, this annual ranking system has almost guaranteed that *SAT* scores are considered the most important factor in college admission. In reality, *SAT* scores remain a notoriously poor measure of both student ability and likelihood of success in college."

For a more thorough discussion of *SATs,* I recommend chapter three of Fox's book *Your Child's Strengths.* But my main concern is that the *SAT,* like general intelligence testing, focuses way too narrowly and leaves many children out who are very talented in ways not measured by this instrument.

Seth Godin writes, "The moment we give up our internal compass in exchange for satisfying the cultural need to follow the leader, we've made someone else boss. In school we teach kids to earn high scores and to comply and to meet the standards of their teachers and parents. But what if those aren't part of *your* agenda?"

Moment of Truth: Before purchasing a college education, clearly identify natural talents and build an education plan around them. Or… develop a great plan that uses college courses to clearly identify passion and aptitude.

"The hiring manager focuses on a resume, which highlights skills acquired through schooling, training, and/or experience. While skills and experience are important attributes that should be considered, talent and passion are even more vital to real job performance success and should be given greater weight."

~Joe Santana, Leadership Coach

CHAPTER 6
Deception: Job Description Confusion

My first career goal was to be a cowboy. Roy Rogers was my first hero and being a cowboy looked cool. The problem was that when I found out what being a "real cowboy" entailed, I didn't like it so much.

I liked the idea of being a hero, having a loyal dog and horse. I had the boots, hat, gun, and dog. But I really was "all hat and no cattle". When I discovered that being a cowboy involved camping with very few *Hampton Inns* or *Starbucks* in sight, I reconsidered my choice. My first efforts on a horse didn't go well either. To this day when I mount a horse, they crane their neck back around and look at me as if to say, "Who is this guy, and what are you doing on my back?" And the idea of jerking a baby calf off its feet at a full gallop, then applying a hot brand to its backside, well, that still just seems wrong to me. Over time, I found that the only rodeo I really enjoyed visiting was Rodeo Drive in Beverly Hills.

A lot of people have false starts like this in their careers. Nicholas Lore explains this very well in his terrific book, *The Pathfinder*. Lore writes, "If you are like most of us, when you attempt to make career decisions, you imagine careers that might be interesting (doctor, lawyer, Indian Chief). Your mind hops from one potentially interesting career to another. Your romantic imagination kicks in. You think of all the positive aspects of the job: 'Let's see, I really like the idea of becoming an Indian Chief. It seems like an exciting job, working outside, nature all around, not a boring desk job, great clothes, etc.' Then after a while, you have an attack of negative considerations, an attack of 'Yeah but' thoughts: 'I'm allergic to feathers, those cold winter nights in the teepee, and what about the cavalry attacks?' You are left with a veritable blizzard of mental images and opinions about potential careers yet are no nearer to making a definite decision about which one to pursue. What's worse, using this method, things tend to get foggier rather than clearer."

Lore continues, "When you first think of a new potential career, it is an idea as pure as newly fallen snow. Then as you think of it more, your opinions, both positive and negative, tend to get stuck onto the original picture. After a while, whenever the thought of that particular career surfaces in your mind, all you see is all the stuff stuck to it. When you think 'Indian Chief,' up pops a picture of a cavalry attack."

I call this the **"Do, Be, Do, Be, Do" Deception**.

We confuse *being* something we imagine is very cool with actually *doing* it. Many times our choice is around fame and fortune. Sometimes we pick a career because we believe that we will be highly esteemed by others.

But strengths strategist Marcus Buckingham rightly observes, **"Doing trumps being every time"**. Similarly, football coach Vince Lombardi used to talk about "loving the daily grind". And essayist Logan Pearsall Smith once wrote, "The test of vocation is the love of the drudgery it involves." There are several ways to **test drive a career** before buying. Many people who wouldn't think of buying a car without a test drive or a suit of clothes without trying it on, think nothing of going into debt for 10's or even 100's of thousands of dollars on an education. I recommend *job shadowing*, which is spending a day or two with a top professional in the field you're considering. If that goes well, pursue an *internship*. We have a family member who is considering medical school. He's a college graduate and has the grades. He's wisely testing the waters. He worked first as an Emergency Medical Technician to see how he handled the blood. Now he's working as a medical scribe in a top hospital to get a feel for the different medical roles. This is so smart. *Volunteering* or otherwise offering your services for free is another way to avoid the "Do-Be-Do" Deception.

Aptitude Testing is an excellent first step and I highly recommend it. But this should be followed with **Activity Testing** using a few of the ideas above.

Most people select career targets before they are clear on what people in a profession actually do on a day-to-day basis. *O*NET* is a resource that provides a reasonably accurate list of professional tasks for over 800 professions. To use this resource, go to www.onetonline.org . In the *Occupation Quick Search*, in the upper right hand corner, type in the name of your target job or profession. You will come to a page of positions that are loosely in your field. Click on the one that is most similar to your career target. This will bring you to a page that displays a sample of reported job titles. I just typed in *Accounting* and came up with 14 professional occupations that are related to this field. Click on any of the 14 occupations and you will be directed to a detailed "Summary Report" on that specific job. A few lines down you'll find "Tasks" with a + symbol. Click on the + and it will expand the tasks. **Here is a modified task list similar to what you might find for accountant:**

• Operate accounting software to record and analyze information
• Check financial documents for correct entry, accuracy and codes
• Classify, record, and summarize numerical and financial data
• Compile and keep financial records
• Enter debit, credit, and total accounts on spreadsheets and databases
• Operate 10-key to produce calculations and documents
• Receive, record, and bank cash, checks, and vouchers
• Comply with federal, state, and company regulations
• Compile financial, accounting or auditing reports and tables
• Record receipts, expenditures, payables, receivables, profit/loss
• Code records according to company procedures
• Reconcile and report discrepancies found in documents
• Access financial information to answer questions
• Match order forms with invoices, and record necessary information
• Perform personal bookkeeping services

- Prepare deposits, verify and balance receipts, sending payments
- Prepare trial balances
- Calculate, prepare, and issue bills, invoices and statements
- Calculate and prepare payments
- Compute deductions for income and social security taxes
- Prepare and process payroll information
- Reconcile printouts and manual journals
- Reconcile bank transactions
- Transfer journal details to general ledger or data sheets
- Complete and submit tax forms and returns
- Prepare workers' comp forms, pension forms, documents
- Prepare purchase orders and expense reports
- Monitor status of loans ensuring payments are up to date
- Calculate amounts due, interest, balances, discounts
- Calculate equity and principal
- Calculate material cost, overhead, expenses, estimates, pricing
- Prepare budget from estimated revenue, expenses and prior budget
- Maintain inventory records
- File, answer phones, handling correspondence

As you read through the list, imagine yourself doing these tasks on a daily basis. If, based on your strengths from the last chapter, you are a good fit for accounting, you might get a burst of energy as you read it. If, like me, you dropped out of accounting in high school and have had a long standing love-hate relationship with *Excel* spreadsheets, you may feel a cold shiver go up your spine. Even thinking about a job in accounting is scarier than a Stephen King novel. If that's you, cross accounting off your list.

Job Shadows

If you get the burst of energy, double check it. Try to set up a job shadow with an accountant friend of the family or walk into an accountant's office, introduce yourself and ask for permission to spend some time observing someone doing the actual work.

Volunteer Work

If the work still excites you, try to get some experience volunteering as a bookkeeper.

Moment of Truth: Make sure to pick a career where the tasks and roles involve activities that is actually enjoyable, generally for long periods of time.

"Don't let your babies grow up to be cowboys... make 'em be doctors and lawyers and such."

~Willie Nelson, Country Music Star

CHAPTER 7
Deception: Parental Advice

Parents aren't the only source of advice in our lives. We get a lot more than we think from Peers (Friends), Partners (Spouses), Professors (Teachers), Pastors/Priests (Ministers), Programs (Television), Promoters (Salespeople) and Professionals (Career Service). Much of this advice will be well intentioned. Much of it will be with our ultimate best interest in mind. Some of it won't be. Some advice will be based on these groups own needs and self interest. Taken as a whole, the body of advice from all these people will be conflicting.

Former *General Electric* CEO Jack Welch and his wife Suzy tell a story in their book *Winning* that represents the parental advice trap very well. A student was about to graduate from *Harvard* and he set up an appointment to get career advice from one of Jack's friends, a woman who was very familiar with investment banking and management consulting. The woman said she answered each question the young man had very thoroughly, and he took good notes. But he wasn't especially curious about anything. After about 30 minutes he thanked her politely and stood up to leave. As he did this, he stuck his note pad inside a folder and she noticed that it was totally covered with very detailed drawings of cars.

"Wow, those are amazing! Who did them?" she asked. **In the blink of an eye the student was full of energy** as he said, "I did—I'm always drawing cars... my dorm room is covered with posters and paintings of cars—I subscribe to every car magazine! I've been obsessed with cars since I was five years old. My whole life, I've wanted to be a car designer. That's why I'm always going to car shows and *NASCAR* races. I went to Indianapolis last year—I drove there!"

Jack's friend tried to convince the student that he actually belonged in Detroit or working for a car company. But she said he deflated just as quickly as he had come to life a few minutes earlier, "My dad says the car business is not what I went to *Harvard* for."

She wasn't surprised when she bumped into the father a few months later and he proudly told her that his son was working 80 hour weeks at a *Wall Street* firm.

Jack Welch continues, "I know someone who literally became a doctor because his entire childhood his mother—a Polish immigrant who loved the American Dream—introduced him by saying, "And here's my doctor!" He didn't hate the profession, but you've never met anyone more eager to retire. Welch summarizes his thoughts with this, "**Working to fulfill someone else's needs or dreams almost always catches up to you**."

Issac Newton followed his inner pull and became a world class physicist, mathematician, astronomer, and theologian. Imagine if he had followed his mother's desire that he run the family farm. **Dvorak** and **Handel** were world class composers. Dvorak's father wanted him to become a butcher and Handel's father hoped that he would pursue law. *Whole Foods* founder **John Mackey's** mother wanted him to go back to college and become a doctor. She thought becoming a grocer was a waste of his potential.

If you are a parent, your role should be one of objectively trying your best to help your child discover their own unique design, passions, talents and then support them relentlessly in their pursuit. If you are a child of a pushy parent, adult or otherwise, it's critical that you respectfully listen to their viewpoint and then go on following the trail of gifts and desires God has placed deep inside.

I love the *Amplified Bible's* translation of Proverbs 22:6, "Train up a child in the way he should go [**and in keeping with his individual gift or bent**], and when he is old he will not depart from it."

There are probably a variety of reasons parents push their kids toward work that is often unsuited for them. Some parents want to continue building their business and legacy. Some parents are trying to live their lives vicariously through their children. If I had a son, I'm sure I would have nudged him pretty hard toward baseball, hoping he could do what I didn't. For some it may be pride, for others security. Mothers may be particularly inclined to push their kids in the direction of jobs that they feel are "secure" especially if a father or a spouse didn't provide what they considered a level of security. Sometimes parents just think they know better. Maybe occasionally they do...

Each new generation provides new challenges for parents. I remember growing up reading the biography of baseball great Ty Cobb who is still on anybody's short list of top players of all time. His father was vehemently against his son playing baseball, believing it to be a complete waste of time with no future. With today's multimillion dollar salaries, most parents take a gentler view of baseball as a career choice today.

But, **what about video gaming, snowboarding and skateboarding?**

What about *MMO* (Massively Multiplayer Online) or *Synthetic Universe* games like *Eve?*

Before you judge too quickly, I recommend *Total Engagement: Using Games and Virtual Worlds to Change the Way People Work and Businesses Compete* by Byron Reeves and J. Leighton Read. **Even if they don't become professional video game players, you may discover that many other careers are already using the skills developed in video games.**

I don't have all the answers. I recognize that some of these new options have sub-cultures that are fraught with danger and if you are a parent you have every right to be concerned. Just be careful you don't let your fear keep your son or daughter from the career God designed them for.

"He's mentally slow, unsociable and adrift forever in foolish dreams."

~ Albert Einstein's Childhood Instructor

CHAPTER 8
Deception: You Can't Do Anything

What is the essential difference between checkers and chess? Many would answer, "Chess is more complicated than Checkers". Surely this is one right answer. But why is it more complicated? One reason is that **there are multiple pieces in chess with each having different abilities to move on the board.** The Rook moves in straight lines. The Bishop moves diagonally and the Knight moves in an "L" shape. In checkers all the pieces are the same. We live in a world that's more similar to chess than checkers and always have. But, it's a little more complicated than that.

I'm sitting in my office/library as I write this. I'm surrounded by hundreds of books on human potential. Most of them can be summed up in two categories. About half fall in the, **"If You Can Dream It You Can Do It"** category. Many of these books I've owned, read and re-read since I was 19 years old. The message is essentially a checkers message, helping the game piece get across the board and become a "King". But in the 1990s, I began to read another kind of human potential book. This more recent half of my library consists of books in the **"You Can Succeed With Your Natural Talents"** category. I see part of my life work as the blending of these two streams. Really, there is an elegant truth in both the checkers and the chess world.

How did you answer when your children popped the **"Santa Claus"** question? Is there a Santa Claus? Even scientists would agree it's next to impossible to prove a negative. My parents answered Socratically with, "What do you think?" I guess it says something about me that as I move into my 60s, I'm still thinking.

How do you answer your child, student or employee when they come to you with their dreams?

If your young employee, an African American working his first job as an ice cream scooper, told you he wanted to become President one day, what would you tell young Barack Obama?

Would you be the movie producer who told a young Harrison Ford he had no future as an actor? Or would I be the Liverpool high school choir director who thought both George Harrison and Paul McCartney had no special talent? Or would we be the Glee Club organizers who rejected Elvis?

In Hoda Kotb's new book, *Where We Belong,* she writes about Michelle, a junior in high school showing up for a meeting with her guidance counselor. She walked into the woman's office and was greeted with the **"So What Do You Want To Be When You Grow Up?"** question. When Michelle answered, "A doctor", the counselor actually snickered and said, "Let's find something more suitable for you to do." The counselor looked through Michelle's file and even though she could see how academically gifted she was, the advice was for her to "find something working in a factory". Michelle had to overcome a lot of roadblocks and detours but today she is a medical doctor.

A college guidance counselor, after seeing a student's first semester grades, recommended that young Ben give up his dream of going to medical school. Instead, Ben did a detailed analysis of his learning style. He carefully considered his successes and failures throughout all his school years. He concluded that his unique learning style showed a strong preference for reading. When the classes were lecture based, he struggled or failed. Ben took radical action. He stopped attending his college classes altogether, hired a note-taker and spent all his days reading the textbooks and the notes. After graduating with honors, Dr. Ben Carson went on to become a brain surgeon assembling a team of over 70 to perform the first successful separation of twins joined at the head.

Melinda says her mom never dissuaded her from trying anything, even if success was unlikely. Her efforts at gymnastics, saxophone and the flute were a disaster. Her real dream was to become a singer, except she was tone deaf. When she auditioned for choir in grammar school she made it because of her charisma, but her singing was so bad she was asked to "lip sync". After telling her mom about dreams of singing like Whitney Houston and her intention of singing at the church talent show, her mom was both supportive and honest. She told Melinda that this would be a great faith project and she would have to both pray and practice REALLY, REALLY, REALLY hard. The talent show day arrived and there was still no evidence she could hit the notes. Melinda walked on stage and incredibly, this beautiful tone came out. Overnight, she could both sing and hear harmonies. After the show, people actually called to complain that the pastor had allowed her to lip sync for the show. The pastor had to convince them it was really Melinda singing. Melinda joined the church worship team and the all-state choir. Then, on season six, Melinda Doolittle walked into an audition for *American Idol*. She was the third place finisher and launched a singing career. For current tour dates and venues go to melindadoolittle.com.

The *Johnson O'Conner Research* offers unique work sample assessments for those who would like some aptitude based guidance on career direction. They have tested hundreds of thousands of people of all ages since their beginnings at a Lynn, Massachusetts *General Electric* laboratory in 1922. Laboratory associate Richard Brehler shares the story of a high school student who wanted to pursue a career in medicine. She had good grades in science and math and an interest profile suggested work in the science and technical area. Her aptitude patterns came back showing low scores for three dimensional visualization and a high score in idea fluency. The student also enjoyed interacting with people and conversation. This mix would not suggest success in medicine. At her assessment debrief she was asked about her reasons for wanting to pursue medicine. Was she wanting to help people? Was she intrigued with surgery or diagnostics? Hmmm… not exactly. She was honest in sharing her interest in the social status and the *Mercedes* that would surely come with the career. She had been influenced by the portrayal of doctors in the movies and on television. She had confused what she wanted to be, a well-respected professional, with what she actually wanted to do.

What do I believe? I believe that the truth is somewhere in the mix of these stories. If you have a dream or passion, pursue it, even if it's a long-shot. If children, students or employees have dreams and passions, encourage them.

Consider natural aptitudes and encourage others to do the same. Consider unique approaches to both learning and work.

And believe… miracles still happen!

"You can be whatever you want to be… A lie. Not everyone can be whatever he or she wants to be. You can become whatever you have the potential to become and are willing to dedicate the time and effort into becoming, and what you have the talent for."

~Larry Winget, The Pit Bull of Personal Development

CHAPTER 9
Deception: You Can Do Anything

If your dream is worthy, one that will genuinely help and serve others, I believe you can be a part of making it happen. I believe you can play some position on that team to realize that dream. I don't know if you are suited to coach, scout, be a statistician, sell season tickets to large corporations, play pitcher or catcher, shortstop or centerfield, sell popcorn in the stands, park cars, be an owner, or a general manager, or announcer in the booth. When the *Chicago White Sox* won the *World Series* in 2005, owner Jerry Reinsdorf saw that every member of the *White Sox* team received the coveted *World Series* ring. Everyone on staff got one, regardless of their position, including the parking lot attendants. Each of the 432 rings handed out were 14 carat gold with 95 diamonds totaling over 2 carats. Jerry Reinsdorf understood like few others, that it takes Team Work to Make the Dream Work!

With that said, let me move on to the deception part....

The idea, "If you can dream it you can do it" may not be uniquely American but it is a huge piece of our natural psyche. This one often comes disguised as "The American Dream". It is the idea that anyone can do anything they want to. Its roots are deeply imbedded in *Tabula Rasa* (Latin: *blank slate*) which refers to the thesis that individual human beings are born with no built-in mental content, in a word, "blank", and that their

45

entire resource of knowledge is built up gradually from their experiences and sensory perceptions of the outside world. It is supported by many psychological theories including American psychologist-educator-inventor-poet B.F Skinner who established his own philosophy called *Radical Behaviorism.*

Skinner believed and taught immediate positive and negative reinforcement. He supported the idea that with proper behavioral objectives and feedback everyone should be able to learn anything and everything. Strengths in Education expert Jennifer Fox suggests this is a philosophy permeating education today. Fox says our system is founded on the belief, "That given the right amount of learning in a small enough dose, everyone can master the entire curriculum."

It only follows that this idea is also deeply embedded in our places of work. Motivational experts who espouse theories like *Neuro-Linguistic Programming* (Brain Language Programming) canonize a primary presupposition, "If one person can do something, anyone can do it." It is rampant in all kinds of sales organizations. Network marketers often teach that with hard work, anyone can be successful at selling.

The problem is that they seem to be ignoring loads of evidence and research that balance and complete the conclusions they present. Let me sum up this faulty body of work based on *Behaviorism*, "Talent and innate aptitude is of very little or no importance when it comes to world class performance. Desire, deliberate practice, and supportive environments over time, lead to world class performance."

In other words, the behaviorists take a checkers position in a chess world! In some ways this simplifies management and throws us back into a world of, "If you're not performing, you either have a bad attitude or aren't working hard or smart enough." The problem is that this line of thinking is simply incomplete and will lead millions to frustration and often failure.

Dr. K. Anders Ericsson is a Swedish psychologist and professor of psychology at *Florida State University* who is recognized by some as one of the world's leading theoretical and experimental researchers on

46

expertise. Ericsson is one of the current leaders spreading the checkers myth. His thoughts on innate talent can be summed up here, "With the exception of fixed genetic factors determining body size and height, we were unable to find evidence for innate constraints to the attainment of elite achievement for healthy individuals."

I believe that educators, Skinner, and a host of motivational speakers have significant value in inspiring people to reach their full potential and I am indebted to many of them. In Ericsson's case he has uncovered some critical details that would help anyone develop innate talent. But again, as I shared in the last chapter, **we must move from the checkers mentality to a chess mentality**. Chess is more complicated than Checkers. There are multiple pieces in chess with each having different abilities to move on the board. We will continue to live in a chess world.

One of my heroes is motivational speaker Zig Ziglar. One of my treasured possessions is a picture of Zig and I when I was receiving a diploma as a graduate of his *Richer Life Course*. I worked in his organization for a year under his vice-president Jim Anders. I owe him a lot in my personal growth and development. Zig rightly inspires us when he says, "Man is designed for accomplishment, engineered for success, endowed with the seeds of greatness." I couldn't agree more. **But we are designed differently, engineered uniquely, and each endowed with seeds that bloom in different shades, colors and hues.**

Dreams Happen When We:
1. **Discover** our unique natural gifts, talents, aptitudes, abilities, traits, and passion.
2. **Develop** those unique natural gifts, talents, aptitudes, abilities, traits, and passion through hard work over time into full-fledged strengths. It is actually in the skill development step that the work of the behaviorists, motivators and Ericsson's work becomes extremely useful.
3. **Deliver** those gifts, talents, abilities, traits, and passion to a place that intersects with a need in the marketplace. When built solidly on the

foundation of natural talents, the development and delivery of those talents become the "heart" of performance.

4. **Describe** and **Demonstrate** our abilities to others on resumes and brochures, in interviews and presentation.

5. **Delegate** our non-strengths to those who have developed their own passion and talents with high levels of knowledge and skill in the areas of our weakness.

In my workshops and classes I often write two statements on the board or flip chart:

You Can't Do Anything
You Can Do Anything

What's the difference?

The difference is the first statement has an **'t** (apostrophe followed by a "t") that the second statement doesn't have. Beyond that they are opposite messages. But I believe they are both lies. They are both serious deceptions.

If you grew up in an environment that pushed the first deception, "You Can't Do Anything", that's a tough one. It may take a while for you to learn that it just isn't true.

The second lie doesn't have the same negative emotional impact. It is probably delivered with all the best intentions. But it's not true, just the same.

So what is true?

Moment of Truth: All Of Us Can Do Amazing Things! Each Of Us Can Do Important Things! We Can Make A Huge Difference With Our One Life! And we'll be the most amazing, contribute the most and make the biggest difference if we spend the majority of our time working from our natural talents.

Note: K. Anders Ericsson has made numerous claims in multiple forums that beyond height and weight, innate talent doesn't exist. For a rigorous scholarly debunking of the questionable research underpinning those claims you might try:

The International Handbook on Giftedness by Larisa V. Shavinina, editor. While I do believe Ericsson is badly mistaken on this fundamental point, his ideas on training and development are exceptional.

"Our talents feel so natural to us that they seem to be common sense."

~Marcus Buckingham, Strengths Strategist

CHAPTER 10
Deception: Anyone Can Do This?

This deception is perhaps the most self-imposed, but it can come from the outside as well. I call it the "self-depreciation" or the "doesn't everyone" deception. Many of us find it very difficult to convince ourselves of our enduring uniqueness. And if we do understand our uniqueness, it's sometimes hard to imagine it being of any value, especially a value that someone would actually pay for. We pause to wonder at the stars, we pause to wonder at the sunset, we pause to wonder at the gifts and talents in others, we might even pause to wonder at the Creator of all those things. And so we should. But we never pause to wonder at ourselves.

Life Strategist Bobb Biehl believes the most common erroneous mistake human beings make is that, "Everyone is basically like me." In *Focusing Your Life* he writes, "No one is like you. It is important to understand yourself, how you are unique, to accept that uniqueness and focus its strength in the direction you want to go. If you assume everyone is like you, you will not be looking for your uniqueness. You will assume that what is hard for you is hard for everyone. You will have no interest in finding what seems second nature to you but seems very difficult or impossible for others. This is the uniqueness upon which you should center your strengths for the future."

Our talents often come so easy to us. In fact, by definition that's part of what actually makes it a talent. As Marcus Buckingham and Don Clifton say in *Now, Discover Your Strengths*, "Our talents feel so natural to us that they seem to be common sense." Doesn't everyone see the world as I do? Doesn't everyone feel a sense of impatience to get this project started? Doesn't everyone want to avoid conflict and find common ground? Can't everyone see the obstacles lying in wait if we proceed down this path?

NO THEY DON'T!!!

Our truth or sense isn't common at all. The sense we make of the world is individual. Our "sense," our recurring pattern of thought, feeling, or behavior is caused by our unique mental network. This network serves as a filter, sorting and sifting the world we encounter, causing us to zero in on some stimuli and miss others entirely.

Sometimes I illustrate this in one of our strengths classes by wadding up some papers and throwing them on the floor. When I ask how many people noticed it, the responses are quite varied. Some don't notice the paper at all. Some notice it but don't think much about it. Others almost have to be tied down to keep them from picking up the paper and messing up the illustration.

Some of our talents are like breathing to us. We just do it without much effort. Some of our passions are so enjoyable it would seem like cheating to get paid for it.

Entrepreneur and author Rajesh Setty says, "Many times we are blind to things that are close to us. Our strengths are one area that we may be blind to. Other people can see our strengths but we can't. When we work from our areas of strength, we achieve success almost effortlessly. When there is no effort, how can you notice it?"

Many years ago in my Psychology 101 class I heard about the *Johari Window* created by Joe Luft and Harry Ingham. If you do a *Google Images* search you will find many dozen versions.

As you can see on the next page, four windows are presented in the *Johari Window* diagram. You will find the meaning of each when applied to talents or strengths.

Open Talents: <u>Everybody</u> **Knows It**. This quadrant represents your talents and strengths that both you are aware of and those around you are aware of.

Hidden Talents: <u>Only You</u> **Know It**. This quadrant represents those talents and strengths that only you are aware of.

Blind Spot Talents: <u>Only They</u> **Know it**. This quadrant represents those talents and strengths we are primarily talking about in this chapter. They are talents that other people can see in us but we struggle to see ourselves.

Unknown: <u>Only God</u> **Knows it**. This quadrant represents those talents and strengths that lie dormant or unknown. It is often because the tasks and activities that you have experienced haven't exposed some of your talents. I also call this the **"God" Quad** because only God is aware of these gifts. Author Max Lucado says, "We suffer from poor I-sight." He suggests that it requires an encounter with God to correct that problem.

The Johari Window

Open	Blind
Hidden	Unknown

Moment of Truth: Talents and passion may seem so effortless and enjoyable we undervalue them.

"I can pull you over like a rubber band, but you'll eventually pull back to what's natural."

~Dr. Phillip McGraw (Dr. Phil)

Chapter 11
Deception: Change Your Personality

This deception is what I call the "changing personality" deception. About 66% of us believe that we can change our basic personality and alter our talent distribution as we get older. The truth is, with regard to our temperament strengths, we don't change much. My first grade teacher commented on how "serious" I was. My wife was concerned on our first date that I might be "too serious for her", and in my last performance appraisal at work, my manager commented on my seriousness and how "it might benefit me to loosen up a bit".

I'm happy to report that I was able to convince my wife that I had a seriously non-serious side. I was able to quickly produce a picture of me dancing on a bar in Las Vegas taken on a company scavenger hunt. I also offered a reasonably professional recording of me singing Johnny Cash's Country hit, *A Boy Named Sue*. I do loosen up once you get to know me, but chances are your first impression of me will be that I'm a fairly intense serious type. That hasn't changed much since first grade.

Columbia University's Nathan Brody once commented in a speech, "Change is the process of becoming more like who we are." Science author William Wright says, "As we age, we tend to become more like the genetic blueprint with which we started in life."

Of course our values may shift slightly and our beliefs may dramatically change. The apostle Paul's dramatic conversion in the Bible was an example of this. He went from encouraging the murder of Christians to becoming one and then to spending his life urging others to become one. His beliefs experienced a dramatic change. But his talents and temperament, the core of who he was, didn't change one bit. He was intense and driven before his conversion. He was intense and driven after his conversion.

Instinctual Drift

Instinct or innate behavior is the inherent inclination of a living organism toward a particular behavior. A simple example of an instinctive behavior is a fixed action pattern, in which a very short to medium length sequence of actions, without variation, are carried out in response to a clear stimulus. We often call this simply, "Stimulus-Response."

Any behavior is instinctive if it is performed without being based upon prior experience and is therefore an expression of innate biological factors. In other words there is an absence of learning.

Newly hatched on a beach, sea turtles will automatically move toward the ocean. A young kangaroo climbs into its mother's pouch upon being born. Honeybees communicate by dancing in the direction of a food source. All this is done without formal instruction.

Instincts and Reflexes

The examples above are complex behaviors and are different from simple reflex behaviors. An instinct should be distinguished from a *reflex,* which is a simple response of an organism to a specific stimulus. An example of a reflex might be the contraction of the pupil in response to bright light or the movement of the lower leg when the knee is tapped (A knee-jerk reaction). By comparison instincts are inborn but more complex patterns of behavior. People can adjust an instinctive behavior or fixed action pattern with awareness and persistence. That does not mean the tendency goes away.

Instinctual drift might be thought of as the tendency to revert to instinctive behaviors that can interfere with conditioned responses. The concept originated with B.F. Skinner's former students Keller and Marian Breland when they tried to teach a pig to put money in a piggy bank. Instead the pig instinctually drifted to its instinctive behavior of putting the money on the ground, as they would do with food.

There is an old saying, "Don't try to teach a pig to sing… It's a waste of your time and it frustrates the pig." Similarly, G.K. Chesterton wrote, "Do not free a camel of the burden of his hump, you may be freeing him from being a camel."

"Everybody is a genius. But if you judge a fish by its ability to climb a tree, it will live its whole life believing that it is stupid."

~Albert Einstein

Chapter 12
Deception: Deficit Attention Disorder

That's not a typo. "Deficit Attention Disorder" is **NOT** Attention Deficit Disorder (ADD) or Attention Deficit Hyperactive Disorder (ADHD). It is a currently unrecognized disorder that may be even more serious.

The deception is this: The majority of us believe that we grow most by fixing our deficits or weaknesses. That is the basis for "Deficit Attention Disorder". We think that in order to grow we should improve a weakness. If we want to help our children, our students, our spouse, or our employees grow we will almost always try to help them overcome or develop a weakness. But this is the wrong focus. If you really want to grow and develop, or help others, choose to develop talents in those areas where great natural ability already exists.

The *Nebraska School Study Council* asked the *University of Nebraska* to launch a major three year study to determine the best way to teach speed reading. In one study on reading enhancement they compared the percentage of improvement contrasting poor readers with gifted readers. The findings included three dramatic conclusions:

1. The best teachers got the best results, independent of who was being taught. This conclusion aligns perfectly with recent research being conducted by the *Gates Foundation*.

2. The second conclusion was not a surprise. The best results came when the best teachers interacted with the best students.

3. The third conclusion was startling to even the most experienced of the researchers. Setting aside who was doing the teaching, going through the same program, poor readers increased their reading speed from 90 to 150 words per minute. That's almost double...not bad. But gifted readers increased their speed from 350 to 2900 words per minute. In a nutshell, the fastest readers grew and profited the most from the training. There is solid biological and neurological underpinnings to this. You come pre-wired to grow exponentially in your natural talents. But again most of us don't believe that.

The assistant director of Cincinnati public schools, George Reavis, wrote a wonderful short story during the 1940s that is, in my experience, a very accurate commentary on our education system. The story begins,

"Once upon a time, the animals got together and decided to start a school. They adopted a full curriculum that was easy to administer and designed to develop a well-rounded animal. There were classes in running, swimming, climbing, jumping and flying.

The duck was a very good swimmer... actually even better than his instructor. He passed flying but only barely, and failed running. Before long he was asked to drop swimming and stay after school so he could practice running. The running practice caused problems with his webbed feet to the point he became only average in swimming. Average was acceptable, so no one worried too much... except the duck.

The rabbit started at the top of his class in running, but he was asked to drop that and stay after class and work harder on his swimming. He developed a nervous twitch from so much swimming, and that negatively impacted his running.

The squirrel was naturally a fantastic climber, but he was constantly frustrated in flying class because his teacher wanted him to start from the ground. He regularly got cramps from over exertion and ended up with only a C in climbing and a D in running.

The eagle was always in trouble for being a non-conformist. In climbing class he beat everyone else to the top of the tree, but he used his own methods for getting there.

Then one day, a wise old owl came to be the new headmaster of school. He re-arranged the curriculum so that ducks could spend most of the time swimming, rabbits could spend most of their time running, squirrels could spend most of their time climbing, and eagles could spend most of their time flying.

The animals went on to get very good high paying jobs doing what they loved and were good at." **The End**

I'm guessing your time in school, like mine, may not have ended that way. "Deficit Attention Disorder" is so ingrained in our culture. We absolutely believe that the path to success is more about fixing our weaknesses than amplifying our strengths. This has been verified by *Gallup Polls* and *Surveys* and can be confirmed in most families where a report card is brought home. Marcus Buckingham regularly tells the story about the proverbial kid who brings home two A's, one C, and one F. Then he rhetorically asks which grade gets the most parental attention. In most every family the answer is the F. Buckingham suggests that the parents role is not to ignore the F but most of the attention should be placed on the A's. My experience is that this suggestion is hugely counter-cultural. Eighty percent of American families would place most of the attention on improving the F.

Leadership author and speaker John Maxwell has a good way of explaining this. He will draw out a graph that looks something like this:

1 2 3 4 5 6 7 8 9 10

Then Maxwell, who authored the book, *Talent Is Never Enough*, goes on to explain,

"You've probably heard somebody say, 'You can do anything as long as you put your mind to it.' Sadly, as nice as that sounds, it simply isn't true. In watching people grow, I have discovered that, on a scale of 1-10, people can only improve about two notches. For instance, I love to sing; that's the good news. The bad news is that I can't carry a tune. Now, let's be generous and say that, as a singer, I'm a 'two'. If I put lots of money, effort, and energy into developing my voice, perhaps I can grow into a 'four'. News flash: on a ten-point scale, four is still below average. With regards to my career, it would be foolish for me to focus my personal growth on my voice. At best, I'd become an average singer, and no one pays for average."

Maxwell continues, "Don't work on your weaknesses. Devote yourself to fine-tuning your strengths. I work exceptionally hard on personal growth in four areas of my life. Why only four: Because I'm only good at four things. I lead, communicate, create, and network. That's it. Outside those areas, I'm not very valuable. However, within those areas of strength I have incredible potential to make a difference."

I have four decades of experience in the workplace. This includes a decade growing up in a family business, a decade founding and building my own small business, a decade working as a sales rep for two large companies and a decade working as trainer and manager for a large company. I have served on the boards of three non-profits across a span of 30 years. All of this experience overwhelmingly confirms everything I have just written - there is a disproportionate focus on weakness in our culture. Most parents, most marriages, the education world, the corporate world and the church world are overwhelmingly and unhealthily concerned with fixing weaknesses. It's not that some of the weaknesses don't need to be fixed. Some do. The problem is the emphasis or focus.

And then there is my experience with golf, by many estimations an intrinsically humiliating sport. I mean come on, the ball just sits there. My experience with golf even suggests that if I'm shooting scores in the mid-eighties, and I work really hard I might actually regress and begin shooting scores in the high nineties. In an area of non-talent, hard work might actually in some cases send you backwards.

Moment of Truth: You will grow most by developing your areas of natural talent!

"As soon as I could afford to hire my weaknesses I did."

~Sara Blakely, founder of Spanx

Chapter 13
Deception: Do Whatever It Takes

Most of us are taught to "do whatever it takes" to help the team win and that includes spending large amounts of time contributing our lesser talents and even our non-talents. In a commercial, basketball star Carmelo Anthony communicates this idea while promoting his version of a new Michael Jordan (*Nike*) shoe, the *M7*. In the commercial, Carmelo plays every position on the court. He is the coach, the janitor, the photographer, and is even in the broadcast booth as the announcer.

On occasion we do need to step up and do something that needs to get done, even if it is outside what we do best and enjoy most. I played high school baseball and during my sophomore year I actually started at seven different positions including catcher, 3rd base, 1st base, 2nd base, shortstop, right field and left field. That year I played everything but pitcher and center field. I was the proverbial "utility player" who could contribute in a variety of positions. Honestly, I really loved that roll! I enjoyed the intellectual stimulation of learning the different positions. I also produced reasonably well with the bat and overall it was a fun year. At the awards banquet I was shocked when I received the coach's award for my contributions.

I've owned a couple of businesses in the construction industry where I was the chief cook and bottle washer. I did everything at times. I can clean the toilets, wash dishes and vacuum at home. So what I'm about to say should never be an issue of pride. You can never believe that you are too good to perform a particular role.

There are occasions when you need to perform in an area that is not a strength. In a tough economy, you may even have to - like financial guru Dave Ramsey suggests, "Deliver a few pizzas." But **the most successful team players stay committed to consistently offering up the best of themselves knowing that their talents will make the biggest contributions to the team's winning on the athletic field or in the marketplace**. This is fairly well understood in athletics but I am amazed at how poorly it's understood in corporate America. Employees are routinely expected to perform in positions and roles they have absolutely no chance to excel in. The reason for this has a lot to do with the next deception we will discuss.

When a "do whatever it takes" mindset means that you must regularly perform in areas that have little or nothing to do with your natural wiring, talent, and aptitude - you need to make an adjustment. That adjustment may mean re-crafting your position, renegotiating your role, and in some cases it may mean looking for another position in different company altogether.

The *Gallup Organization* has exhaustive research that suggests over eight out of ten workers don't have the opportunity to do what they do best everyday. Of those eight out of ten it is suggested that 1/3 of the workers are in the ballpark of their strengths but they would be far more effective if they were doing a reduced subset of their current work. Another 1/3 would be far more effective if they had expanded duties around their current work. The remaining 1/3 would be far more effective in another role or position altogether.

If you want to maximize your performance and your paycheck, if you want to maximize you success and your satisfaction, you must become a 20 percenter. A 20 percenter is a person that works in a role that allows them to do what they do best everyday. It is so named because at most, only 20 percent of the work force falls into this category. You must craft and build and negotiate your tasks and roles so that they fit you succinctly.

Moment of Truth: The most selfless thing an individual can do is stay focused on consistently offering up their talents while maximizing contribution to the team, the organization and even the country.

"People believe you need to be well rounded and work on your weaknesses. That's just not true. To compete on a world class level, you need to accentuate your strengths. Focus on the things you're good at and let someone else do the rest."

~Robert Herjavec

CHAPTER 14
Deception: Work On Your Weakness

Okay, I admit it. I like the Clint Eastwood *Dirty Harry* movies. Part of my attraction to Clint Eastwood and many of the characters he plays on film is a basic no-nonsense, no-talk introversion.

I know Eastwood's most iconic line is, "Go ahead, make my day." But my favorite is really a strengths line, "A man's got to know his limitations." I believe it was delivered in the *Magnum Force* film. If you missed the movie, you can see Eastwood delivering the line on an 11 second *YouTube* clip. If you'd like, feel free to pull it up on *Google* and watch it before returning to the book. You have my permission.

From a strength's perspective, it is every bit as important to avoid using your non-talents on a consistent basis as it is to maximize your talent use. Jay Niblick in his brilliant book, *What's Your Genius?* tackles this subject very effectively. Jay says, "A non-talent isn't really a weakness until you begin depending on it for success. The key is that weaknesses are not natural, they are manufactured. When you allow your success to depend on your talents, you create strengths. When you allow your success to depend on your non-talents, you actually create weaknesses. You are in control."

During the 20th Century, no one had more impact on professional management thinking and practice in this country than Peter Drucker. He phrased Jay Niblick's thoughts in a different way when he said, "Your job is to make your strengths effective and your weaknesses irrelevant."

We are a country obsessed with balance and overcoming weakness in both education and the corporate world. We are often encouraged to overcome our non-talents by trying to become competent at everything. It's not possible or desirable. Successful people aren't well-rounded, they're pointy.

I love what leadership author and speaker John Maxwell says about his own limitations. Maxwell says, "I am worthless in most things. But there are 4 things I do very well! And those 4 things give me huge return.

Leadership - I spend a lot of time leading.
Communication - I teach, I speak a lot.
Create - Writing - I spend a lot of time creating, writing books and so on.
Networking - Relating with other people."

If you're keeping a "Strengths or Career Design" Notebook, add a section on Non-Talents and begin making a list of those things you are just not naturally very good at.

The STRENGTHSPATH philosophy is about minimizing time spent on weaknesses and neutralizing them. Tiger Woods is arguably one of the best golfers to ever play the game. Whether or not he will be the best of all time is yet to be decided in the coming years on the golf course. What's helpful is his approach to strengths and weaknesses on the golf course. The year 2000 was his best year on tour of any to date. He played 76 tournament rounds and 1368 holes of golf that year. He had nine victories in 20 starts, three of them majors, including the 15-stroke mindblower at *Pebble Beach* and an eight shot runaway at the *British Open*. Add the unforgettable playoff triumph over Bob May at the *PGA* and you've got the anatomy of the greatest year in golf history. Tiger finished outside the top five just three times all season, never worse than a tie for 23rd at the *Western Open*. He won $9,501,387 in tournament prize money in that single year.

What's just as amazing are the categories he wasn't the best in. Even during what was arguably the best year by any golfer in tour history, Tiger still had weaknesses. He was 65th in avoiding three putts. He was 54th in driving accuracy percentage. He was 59th hitting greens in regulation from off the fairway. He was 36th in putts per round. He was only 24th in total birdies. He was 51st in sand save percentage.

On that last statistic, it's fairly well known that Tiger isn't the best sand player. Some would argue he could be even better if he spent more time on his sand play. But that isn't so. First, the other parts of Tiger's short game is good enough that he doesn't end up in a sand trap that often. Second, he would have to give up the time he spends on his strengths.

Another great golfer Jack Nicklaus recently said, "I never practiced my short game." If you follow golf, this is heresy. Most of the instruction books and videos insist that the short game is the most important part of golf. But Tiger and Jack both practiced just enough on their weaknesses to be competent. Where they both excelled was maximizing their unique strengths on the golf course.

What does all that mean to you?

First, make sure you are in the right role for your natural strengths, especially your talent and temperament. Don't keep playing golf if tennis is your best game. Don't stay in sales if your talents lie elsewhere. Then, within that game that fits you best, identify that very specific niche that suits you. Spend most of your time on that. If there are a few things you are only competent at, fine. That's not a problem. Just keep refining and focusing on what you do best.

Stop It - Crop It - Swap It - Shop It

You can **stop** some weakness or non-talent based activities altogether and no one will even notice. Try it. In some cases you might want to ask permission. In other cases just stop and see what happens. If no one says anything, don't look back.

Some weakness based activities you can **chop** or **crop**. When you're editing, matting or framing pictures you crop it down to what's important. Great photography is often in the art of cropping, of what you leave out. It's the same with making movies. Life and work is no different. You can reduce some activities. Maybe you can't stop it altogether but you can cut down the amount of time you spend on it. This frees up time to spend on those things you are insanely great at.

You can **swap** some weakness based activities. Some things have to get done and get done well. Find someone that is gifted and talented to do what you hate and what you are not good at. William Faulkner, Earnest Hemingway and multitudes of other brilliant authors have been poor at spelling and syntax. What they are insanely great at is getting their thoughts on paper and crafting wonderful word pictures. They employed editors to manage their weaknesses.

Great Gatsby author F. Scott Fitzgerald was a notoriously poor speller. Jane Austin was poor at both spelling and grammar.

The iconic symbol of genius, Albert Einstein, was a bad speller in both English and his native German. He often complained about being poor at math as well. He wasn't but he did keep people around him that were stronger in math than he was.

Winston Churchill was a prolific writer who spelled poorly throughout his career.

Aren't *Renaissance* people good at everything? Apparently not. Leonardo Da Vinci was the poor speller who wrote, "You should prefer a good scientist without literary abilities than a literate one without scientific skills."

Agatha Christie has been sited by the *Guinness* people (world records not Irish beer) as being the best selling author of all time. As she puts it, "I was always the slow one in the family. I was an extraordinarily bad speller and have remained so..."

John F. Kennedy was the notoriously poor speller that was outed by his wife Jackie who went on to become a book editor.

W.B. Yeats actually won the *Nobel Prize* for Literature. Surely he was a good speller. Nope. To see examples of his mistakes take a look through his letters that are littered with misspellings like "feal" for "feel" and "sleap" for "sleep".

Novelist John Irving was so poor at spelling that he was actually turned over to the school psychiatrist for treatment. He reflects on this in one of his more famous novels, *The World According to Garp.* He wrote there, "English is such a mishmash of different languages that no one should ever feel stupid for being a bad speller."

Ben Franklin was not only a bad speller but apparently he wasn't good at taking responsibility for his weaknesses either. He blamed the alphabet! Warren Buffett has often talked about how terrible he would be at philanthropy, at giving away his vast wealth to good causes. He suggests that philanthropy is way too important to be left to someone like him. So he partners with Bill and Melinda Gates. They love philanthropy and are very good at it.

Shouldn't a great business person be reasonably adept at accounting? Not if billionaire Richard Branson who has started and overseen literally several hundred successful businesses is a fair benchmark. Long after he made the fortune, his chief financial officer was still trying to explain to him the difference between net and gross sales, arguably the most elementary concept in all of accounting.

Susy and I have done this very well at home and on projects where we have worked together. We are gifted differently. She is a very creative cook. I clear the table and do clean up. And I'm pretty good at that. I'm fast and efficient. She is brilliant with stewardship of resources. I love to write and she is extremely gifted as an editor.

Sometimes there are activities that everyone on the team is either bad at or hates. Then it's time to **shop** for an outsourced professional. You trade some of your hard earned cash for their passion and talent. Susy and I do that with a part of our yard work. We both hate mowing. My parents started doing this with housework when I was in high school. You don't always have to be wealthy to have someone come in once a month and do some damage control. This applies equally at the office and at home. All you have to sell is your time. The more time you can spend, investing your unique talent and temperament, the more successful you'll be on every level.

Do you have non-talents? Are you a flop at some things...? So is everyone else. But you will be successful by focusing on your strengths, not eliminating all weaknesses. Here's a review of this chapter:

Stop - Don't do it anymore and see what happens.

Crop - Try cutting away the part of the activity that relies on a non-talent.

Swap - Find a partner or outsource the activity.

Shop - Go hire a professional.

Let me offer one last caveat or a bit of a warning. Discovering, developing and delivering your STRENGTHSPATH is not an excuse for bad behavior. Having "Sensitivity" on your list of non-talents doesn't mean you can snap at people or be rude. "That's just the way I am, you'll have to accept me" isn't an excuse.

The STRENGTHSPATH philosophy is also not a reason to dump mundane tasks on others. Making the office coffee, cleaning your dirty dishes and tidying up is everyone's job regardless of natural talent. As one of my clients said, "It's called pitching in."

Most jobs require doing some things we aren't passionate about or particularly good at. Sometimes you just have to suck it up and do something even though it's not in your strengths mix.

Consultant Steve Roesler talks about what happens when a good principle is turned into a rule. A book title, a training program or company initiative gets turned into a buzzword or an iron clad rule that doesn't allow for flexibility. Common sense gets thrown to the wind.

Roesler says, "It's a lot easier to say 'It's all about Strengths' than it is to live a life identifying and acknowledging our strengths; figuring out where we need to become at least adequate in some of our weaknesses; and respecting the people around us enough to behave unselfishly even when we 'feel' like doing our own thing our own way."

Roesler continues, "When we hide behind Strengths as an excuse for bad behavior, we're really saying 'I don't respect you enough to bother to honor you with good behavior.' And when mundane tasks are dumped on someone else because 'I'm not good at it,' then I better ask myself just how I'm using my position power. Is one of my less attractive 'strengths' the inclination to take advantage of others' weakness?"

This is where your character strengths, which are largely about making good choices come into play. Again, the STRENGTHSPATH philosophy is not just about handing off all the rotten jobs to everyone else. If you lean that direction it's time for a character check. It's about contributing your best, your unique contributive advantage, in service of others.

*"Homonyms are words that **sound** alike but have different **meanings**. Homographs are words that are **spelled** the same and have different **meanings**. Heteronyms are a type of homograph that are also **spelled** the same and have different **meanings**, but **sound** different."*

~magickeys.com

CHAPTER 15
Deception: Divisions and Definitions

If you find yourself confused, bored or just sitting there with your eyes glazed over after reading this chapter, I've successfully made my point!

One of the biggest challenges in any field is communication. Part of the problem is that words don't really have precise meanings. But people have precise meanings... sometimes. Put another way, every person means something slightly different even when using the same word. Even dictionary definitions vary. And most dictionaries offer multiple definitions for the same word. And then there is voice inflection and context. My old mentor Zig Ziglar would use the following example:

I Didn't Say He Kissed His Wife.

That seems straight forward enough. It's seven very simple words with generally well understood meanings. But by changing only your emphasis and voice inflection, you can get seven different meanings. Let's try it.

I didn't say he kissed his wife. It may have been said. Somebody else may have said it. You must have heard it somewhere else. But I was not the one to say it.

I **didn't** say he kissed his wife. The focus shifts to pure denial.

I didn't **say** he kissed his wife. I may have written it. I may have inferred it. I may have implied it. But I didn't say it.

I didn't say **he** kissed his wife. Somebody else may have kissed her. I'm really not sure who kissed her.

I didn't say he **kissed** his wife. I said nothing about kissing. They may have hugged or held hands. I saw no kissing.

I didn't say he kissed **his** wife. Maybe it was somebody else's wife. I'm not really sure.

I didn't say he kissed his **wife**. He may have kissed his girlfriend. He may have kissed the person he was with that night.

The Language of Strengths and the Dictionary

John Carroll, in his book *Human Cognitive Abilities,* dives into this problem at great length in his first chapter. Carroll writes, "Although the term ability is in common usage both in everyday talk and in scientific discussions among psychologists, educators and other specialists, its precise definition is seldom explicated or even considered… Frequently, it is used to characterize attributes of human individuals as in expressions like athletic ability, musical ability and cognitive ability. It expresses a kind of potential… Oddly enough, dictionaries are of little help in developing an exact, analyzed meaning of the term. The *American Heritage Dictionary*, for example, defines ability as 'the quality of being able to do something; the power to perform.' Dictionary definitions often have an air of circularity, as is the case here: ability being defined as 'being able to perform something' but able is defined as meaning, 'having sufficient ability'. Dictionaries of psychology might be more useful, but it happens that the word ability does not appear either as an entry term or in the index of a recently issued *Encyclopedia Dictionary of Psychology* although it is used there in numerous contexts, for example, in defining intelligence as the 'all-round mental ability or thinking skills.'"

Carroll goes on for several more pages outlining some of the definition problems in the world of defining, abilities, aptitudes and other words in the world of strengths assessment.

The Language and Terminology of Strengths

Whether you know it or not, there exists several different strengths movement families or groups. Often the proponents of these strength families are obsessed with their particular group or method of explaining strengths. In many cases they are ignorant of the contributions made by other groups. My first exposure to strengths was a very narrow vein of the Four Quadrant Personality Framework. It was based on the ideas of Hippocrates who taught the idea that there were four basic types of people – Choleric, Sanguine, Phlegmatic and Melancholy. For many years I had no idea there were other strength worlds to explore. In some cases, an individual strength group promoter, teacher or trainer doesn't want to admit the existence of other groups because they don't want to introduce competition with a product or series of products they are trying to sell. **One of the things that's unique about my work is that I introduce my readers and listeners to a broad range of strengths ideas, concepts and systems.**

Here are just a few examples of strength family groupings.

Four Quadrant Personality Frameworks

This is usually represented by a simple personality assessment. The most popular is called *D.I.S.C.* which stands for Dominance, Inducement, Submission and Compliance, although various versions may use different words. There are literally hundreds of versions and vendors who provide iterations of this personality assessment and framework. And there are off-shoots like *Social Style Awareness* which is used by sales organizations to help their representatives be more versatile in their communication styles. To our point for this chapter, each of the four letters in *D.I.S.C.* represents a different personality style. But different versions of *D.I.S.C.* plug in different words for each letter. The meanings between different versions of *D.I.S.C.* are similar, but they are not exactly the same. The *D.I.S.C.* framework was designed by psychologist William Marston, who was also the creator of *Wonder Woman* and the polygraph lie detector test. Marston's work on *D.I.S.C.* is a modern version of Hippocrates framework. Industrial psychologist Walter Clarke was probably the first to turn *D.I.S.C.* into an assessment in the 1950s.

16 Type Personality Framework

Myers-Briggs is the most common of the 16 Type Personality Style frameworks. But there are now many versions with slight differences. Most still use the *Myers-Briggs* words and identifying letter sequence, but some don't. Here is the *Myers-Briggs* terminology:

Introvert – Extrovert

Sensor – Intuitive

Thinker – Feeler

Perceiver – Judge

Most of us have a basic idea on what is meant by the Introvert – Extrovert continuum. These terms are fairly common in our culture. The Thinker – Feeler continuum may be a little more difficult, but still reasonably easy to grasp. The Sensor – Intuitive continuum is a bit harder and the Perceiver – Judge concept is much more difficult. I first took the *Myers-Briggs* when I was in my twenties. I came out an INTJ which stands for Introvert- Intuitive-Thinker-Judge. I've studied the framework for 40 years and I feel like I'm finally getting a grasp of it. I think it's a very useful concept, but a little difficult to understand, partially because of the words used to frame it.

Enneagram Framework

The *Enneagram* has grown in popularity in recent years. Again there are many assessments and many variations of this framework. Each places you in one of nine personality types along with a representative 1-9 number label. The specific names vary some but here is an overview of the system from the *Enneagram Institute*:

1- The Reformer

Rational, Idealistic, Principled, Purposeful, Self-Controlled, Perfectionistic

2- The Helper

Caring, Interpersonal, Demonstrative, Generous, Pleaser, Possessive

3- The Achiever

Success-Focus, Pragmatic, Adaptive, Excelling, Driven, Image-Conscious

4- The Individualist

Sensitive, Expressive, Dramatic, Self-Absorbed, Temperamental

5- The Investigator

Intense, Cerebral, Perceptive, Innovative, Secretive, Isolated

6- The Loyalist

Committed, Security-Oriented, Engaging, Responsible, Anxious

7- The Enthusiast

Busy, Fun-Loving, Spontaneous, Versatile, Distractible, Scattered

8- The Challenger

Powerful, Dominating, Confident, Decisive, Willful, Confrontational

9- The Peacemaker

Easygoing, Self-Effacing, Receptive, Reassuring, Agreeable, Complacent

Talent Frameworks

Personality and talent frameworks have some overlap in places but they are essentially different. But, like personality, the talent world has its own groups and way of seeing the world of work through that lens.

Strengthsfinder's Work Approach Talent Framework

When *Gallup*, the provider of the *Strengthsfinder* assessment, talks about strengths they define it as "a consistent pattern of near perfect performance". The *Strengthsfinder* assessment really measures what I call "Approach Talents". In other words, it doesn't so much assess what you do well, as "how you most naturally approach" any type of activity.

Strengthsfinder measures 34 Talent Themes. Each Talent Theme fits into one four Talent Domains. The four Domains are very similar to the four quadrants in the *D.I.S.C.* personality system.

Recognizing the language and terminology problem inherent in the strengths movement, *Gallup* proceeded to legally trademark much of the language it uses including the names of each of the 34 Talent Themes it introduces. In a sense, the trademarking provided a fixed definition of the language. *Gallup*, in effect, created its own dictionary and definitions as far as the strengths movement goes.

The problem is with *Gallup's* use of the word "talent". They have a particular definition of talent. But as we'll see in a few paragraphs, there are other definitions of talent and these other definitions address some work issues that *Gallup* doesn't attempt to cover with *Strengthsfinder*. By their own admission, *Gallup's Strengthfinder* does not attempt to deal with the world of career selection. This assessment is primarily focused on the application of job shaping. In other words, *Strengthsfinder's* central focus is helping people identify how they most naturally approach a task. It doesn't pretend to focus much on what task or type of task an individual should be focusing on, given their unique set of talents. *Strengthsfinder* is a brilliantly crafted tool. In my opinion, everyone should take it and have a 1-34 debrief by a *Gallup* certified coach. But to get a full understanding of one's talent, two or three other assessment approaches are extremely useful.

The *Strengthsfinder* assessment was originally crafted by Don Clifton and Marcus Buckingham. After Clifton's death, Buckingham left *Gallup*, formed his own company and designed a simplified, 9 Theme framework called *StandOut*. It's an excellent tool for those who find 34 Themes just too difficult to get their head around.

Buckingham's Work Activity Talent Framework

When Buckingham left *Gallup*, he tweaked some terminology. He downplayed *Gallup's* definition of strength – "consistent pattern of near perfect performance" and exchanged it for, "An activity that makes you feel strong." In some ways he left the world of objective performance and entered the world of personal feelings. But he also exchanged the focus on talent as a way of approaching work and exchanged it for a focus on specific activities. In his book, Go Put Your Strengths To Work, he encouraged the Love It - Loathe It exercise. He encouraged readers to write out all of their work activities, placing them in either the Love It column or the Loathe It column. I do a similar exercise with three columns, encouraging clients to place their activities in the Awesome column, the Average column or the Awful column.

This focus on specific tasks and activities is a great addition to the Talent discussion. There are some activities you dislike and/or perform poorly at, even when using your best Strengthsfinder approach.

Johnson O'Connor's Work Aptitude Talent Framework

A third definition of talent lies in the word Aptitude. The Johnson O'Connor Foundation was born out of research originally conducted at the Lynn, Massachusetts General Electric plant in the 1920s. O'Connor tested the underlying Aptitudes for particular kinds of work like clerical, working with numbers, producing ideas, musical talent, color perception and structural visualization. While Gallup's Strengthsfinder and Buckingham's Standout assessments are based on self-reported conclusions, O'Connor's assessments were carefully crafted work samples or timed tests of performance. These work sample assessments, testing for aptitude in about 20 categories, are done in 10 major cities across the U.S. The essence of the testing is also done by the Ball Foundation with Career Vision and the Aptitude Inventory Measurement Service (AIMS). The Highlands Ability Battery offers an online version of this testing. YouScience also offers an online version at a very affordable price and I use this with my clients. To further the point of this chapter, none of these organizations use the same words to describe essentially the same aptitudes or talents.

The talent triangle of Approach Talents, Activity Talents and Aptitude

83

Talents all have a critical place in helping an individual discover or create a role that fits. But for the most part, the practitioners of these three very different ways of thinking about talent don't acknowledge each others existence. That's unfortunate. Most of us could benefit greatly from all three ways of thinking about talent. Most organizations would benefit as well.

Edwin Fleishman, *O*NET* and Abilities

I wish the confusion stopped there but it doesn't. Edwin Fleishman's work on *Human Abilities* is a brilliantly outlined explanation of an individual's enduring attributes and capabilities for performing a particular class of tasks. Fleishman's work on abilities is used extensively on the *Occupational Information Network* or *O*NET* which was established in 1992 by the *Department of Labor*.

Essentially the abilities Fleishman describes are aptitudes. There are 52 of these talents and are well described in Fleishman's *Handbook of Human Abilities*. Fleishman and *O*NET* both include abilities like physical strength, coordination, psychomotor and many more. While Fleishman describes and points to individual assessments for most of his 52 abilities, he never put together a widely available testing or assessment system that the general public can access. This is unfortunate because he digs into some nooks and crannies of talent that others don't.

In my own work, I've combined O'Connor's system with Fleishman's and added in a few strays. It produces an extremely comprehensive view of aptitudes classified by 6 Talent types, 31 Talent Themes and over 100 Talent Threads.

Howard Gardner's *Multiple Intelligence Theory*

Some in the educational community have gravitated toward *Harvard University* professor Howard Gardner's *Multiple Intelligence Theory*. It includes eight - Linguistic Intelligence, Math/Logic Intelligence, Spatial Intelligence, Bodily/Kinesthetic Intelligence, Inter-personal Intelligence, Intra-personal Intelligence, Musical Intelligence and Naturalistic

Intelligence. Gardner's criteria for inclusion as an intelligence includes:

1. Potential for isolation during an event ending in brain damage... For example, linguistic abilities can be compromised or spared by strokes.
2. The existence of prodigies, savants and other exceptional individuals... Such individuals permit the intelligence to be observed in isolation from other intelligences.
3. An identifiable set of operations... Musical intelligence, for instance, consists of sensitivity to melody, harmony, rhythm, timbre, texture and musical structure.
4. A developmental history within an individual along with a definable nature of expert performance... One examines the skills, for example, of an expert athlete, salesperson or naturalist, as well as the steps to attaining such expertise.
5. An evolutionary history and evolutionary plausibility... One can examine forms of spatial intelligence in mammals or musical intelligence in birds.
6. Support from tests in experimental psychology... Researchers have devised tasks that specifically indicate which skills are related to one another and which are different.
7. Support from psychometric findings... Batteries of tests reveal which tasks reflect the same underlying factor and which do not.
8. Susceptibility to encoding in a symbol system... Codes such as language, arithmetic, maps and logical expression, among others, capture important components of respective intelligences.

Richard Bolles – What Color Is Your Parachute?

Richard Bolles passed away in 2017 at the age of 90. He was a career counseling national treasure. He reportedly worked with over 40,000 individuals and his book, *What Color Is Your Parachute,* helped millions. But Bolles seems to have avoided the question of natural talent altogether. In the latest editions of *Parachute* (It's updated every year), it reads, "What are skills? We all have three kinds of skills – abilities, talents or whatever you want to call them."

Note: Richard Bolles' *"Parachute"* work is being taken over by his son Gary.

Conclusion

If your eyes are glazed over or you're rolling your eyes about now, I've made my point... you understand the problem.

All of these systems with their unique ways of looking at work and human performance have merit. But I've really just scratched the surface in naming a few of the most common or well-known systems. One of the problems created by so many different viewpoints is a lack of common language around strengths. This language difference makes it much harder to learn about yourself and what careers might be the best fit. It also makes it much more difficult for employers trying to figure out the selection and hiring puzzle.

"If you are truly interested in a No-Limit life, you have to accept that the only kind of work you are interested in is work at its best or highest in all senses, and that your ability to make all your work activities into play has to come first."

~Dr. Wayne Dyer

CHAPTER 16
Deception: False Dichotomy

A final challenge our culture provides us with is the dichotomy difficulty. In general, our culture is driven by putting situations, things and people into clear categories. Circumstances are either good or bad. People are innocent or guilty, sick or healthy, strong or weak, childish or mature, lazy or ambitious, secure or insecure and so on. One of those dichotomies is Work and Play.

We often view work as hard, difficult, drudgery and something we have to do. On the other hand we see play as easy, fun and something we get to do. Especially in the last century, there was talk of the working class and the leisure class. Many of us see play as a reward for finishing our work. We have sayings built around this work/play separation.

"Work Hard – Play Hard"

"The Fun's Over... Time To Get Back to Work"

"All Work and No Play Makes Jack a Dull Boy"

"You've Got Easy Now... But When You Grow Up You'll Have to Work"

When I was coming into my early teens, I remember my mom telling me that I needed to learn "how to work". I interpreted this to mean that work was not pleasant, difficult and something I needed to learn to cope with. Clearly, that's the cultural bent. If that's your expectation, it's much more likely to be your experience. If that's the only story you're told, it's much more likely to be the story you'll live.

We all need to learn "How to Work". But not in the way most of us have been taught. What we all desperately need to be taught, is how to do the work of discovering what work activities we enjoy and can do with great excellence, while making big contributions to others.

In the first section of this book, I quoted Warren Buffett's son Peter. This idea is so important I'm going to insert it here a second time.

"Some people believe that having a good work ethic equates with a willingness to slave away for sixty or eighty hours a week, at a job for which one has no passion for or even actively hates. The idea here is that the sheer effort, self-denial, and time logged on the clock are somehow intrinsically virtuous. That's not virtue; it's masochism! In some cases it's also, paradoxically, a sign of laziness and lack of imagination. If you're such a hard worker, why not use some of that effort and some of those hours to find something you actually like? The essence of a good work ethic starts with meeting a challenge of self-discovery, finding something you love to do, so that work – even, or especially, when it is difficult and arduous – becomes joyful, maybe even sacred."

Most of your job should be enjoyable. If it's not, you're either doing it wrong, have failed to shape it or you're in a job you are not cut out for.

In his insightful blog post, Charlie Gilke writes, "From an early age, we've associated 'work' with something we don't want to do and 'play' with things we want to do. Our lives are structured around 'work' days, 'vacation' and 'leave' days, and 'rest' days. The end result is that we create conceptual dichotomies along the following axes: job/fun, work/play, and leisure/productivity.

But what happens when our work becomes play? Or when our play becomes work? That is, what happens when we find ourselves in the position such that the things we want to do *are the same things* that put food on the table?

What happens is that most people are still stuck with the work/play paradigm that the rest of us are in. On one level, they know that they love what they do, yet at the same time they have to untangle their emotional associations when they talk and think about what they do.

So pernicious is our cultural socialization that it's hard for us to really come to grips with the fact that *it's possible to have fun doing the work that you do* and there's absolutely nothing wrong with that. In fact, that's the ideal situation."

Dr. Wayne Dyer asks the question, "How did this absurd dichotomy originate in the first place? How did some people come to accept that there is work and there is play, and that you have to spend most of your time working so that you can enjoy the rest of your time (as much as you can afford) playing, that play is the reward for 'hard work,' and so on?"

Dr. Dyer goes on to answer his own question, or at least make some suggestions, "I imagine for most of us it started in school, with parents who insisted that their children had to start early to 'work' around the house, assigned them numerous 'jobs,' all the while conveying what a horror it was to wash the dishes or cut the grass. Perhaps they told the children if they wanted to live in the family they had to put in their share of the work, justifying their policies on the basis that they were really just getting their children ready for the way school, or life, 'really is.' But for most of us it very likely started with school, with teachers calling certain times 'play periods' and making certain we knew that when class was in session the teacher was boss again, and that there was no reason for us to expect to enjoy ourselves, because this was work time – time to be conditioned to the idea that work and play were very, very different."

I think there is a religious component to the separation of work and play as well. For many, the story of work begins and ends with man's sin, subsequent fall and the cursing of work. Growing up in the church, this was a backdrop for at least some of my ideas about work.

But that is a woefully incomplete view of the Jewish and Christian Scriptures. To begin with, work clearly did not begin with the fall. In the *Genesis* story, Adam and Eve were working before the fall. And they were doing that work in something like paradise, a place referred to as The Garden of Eden.

From a Christian perspective, Jesus' death and resurrection was the beginning of the end of the curse. The people that I listen to in the Christian faith believe that part of our purpose is to bring Heaven to Earth. We are to participate in the restoration of life as it was in the garden. Perhaps we have a ways to go, but theologically, I think we are standing on very solid ground when we try to infuse our work with play.

The new wave of "Grit Psychology" may also be responsible for keeping the work/play dichotomy in play for the foreseeable future. Grit is clearly an important component of success. The ability to push through difficulties with perseverance is part of any victory worth having. But I fear many are focusing on the persistence element without the passion element. As Grit Psychologist Angela Duckworth says, **"Nobody works doggedly on anything for years if they don't already have an intrinsic interest in it. The people who find and follow their passions tend to be grittier."**

Section II

Circumstances

In this second section we'll look at career difficulties that are largely situational or circumstantial. Maybe you're not in the wrong career, you're just going through a rough patch. This is perfectly normal and requires discipline and determination. It also requires some discernment. There is such a thing as a dead end and a dead horse. With a dead end you must turn around and go a different direction. With a dead horse, the proper thing to do is dismount. With a delay, you must be patient or look for a different path. A delay is not the same thing as a denial.

"The Dip is the long slog between starting and mastery."

~Seth Godin

CHAPTER 17
Dips – Dead Ends – Dead Horses

Seth Godin has a wonderful little book called *The Dip*. It describes a version of what is often called the *Hero's Journey*. Most movies and novels explore some version of the *Hero's Journey* as do many Bible stories. *The Lord of the Rings* and *Harry Potter* both generally follow this "Epic Story" template. *The Hero's Journey* is where fact and fiction collide. In some respect, this pathway is part of everyone's story and it's part of your STRENGTHSPATH. It looks something like this:

Step 1: Sweet Stability. Status Quo is where most stories begin. Everything is going along normally...

Step 2: The Call is what happens next. "Your mission, should you decide to accept it...." You begin a new adventure. You start the book. You begin the new job.

Step 3: The Start is the beginning of the journey. Everything looks great the first week, the first month, the first quarter. All is going according to plan.

Step 4: Then Boom...The Dip is where the challenge begins. The opposition shows up. You lose your job. Sometimes the dip gets deeper and goes on for some time. Sometimes a series of dips come in tight sequence or all together. This is also called the test. Lance Wallnau appropriately refers to the dip as "The Period of Contradiction". Some call it "Death of a Vision". The Scriptures call it "The Valley of the Shadow of Death".

One of my favorite cartoons growing up was *Mr. Wizard and Tooter the Turtle*. Tooter would go off on adventures, get in big trouble and then yell for Mr. Wizard to save him. Mr. Wizard would always use the spell, "Drizzle Drazzle Druzzle Drome, time for this one to come home." Sometimes I feel like Tooter.

Step 5: The Allies show up. Resources, people and money come on the scene. The calvary is coming. Sometimes it comes in the form of a new idea. Sometimes it comes in the form of a new employee or a friend.

Step 6: The Breakthrough happens. The goal is accomplished and you are transformed in the process.

Step 7: You Celebrate. Party!

Step 8: Do it all again!

The Dip is part of your STRENGTHSPATH. No matter how well your assignment fits your natural strengths, it doesn't remove the dip.

What staying on your STRENGTHSPATH does do is make sure that you are working in a place where you are the most creative and the most resilient. You won't avoid dips but you will be much more effective dealing with them. You will experience some defeats on your STRENGTHSPATH. But you will bounce back from each of those defeats much more quickly.

Dead Ends and Dead Horses

Now I want to tee up a related but different topic. I want to talk about dead ends and dead horses. You may experience times in your career that a whole industry folds underneath you. I've had this happen twice.

This will possibly happen to you at least once in your career. It's actually becoming more likely all the time because change is accelerating in most industries. Dead horses are different than dips and it sometimes takes discernment to tell the difference. But you need to decide if you're in a dip or riding a dead horse. If you're in a dip, stay the course or make the needed adjustments. If you're on a dead horse, the only thing to do is dismount and find another horse. Change careers. Change companies. Beating a dead horse is never useful. Neither is beating a sick horse. The smart thing to do is dismount.

This is the brilliance of Seth Godin's book *The Dip*. He offers some wisdom, encouragement and discernment to help you tell the difference between dips and dead horses. And he gives you permission to quit when you have, in fact, identified that you're riding the dead horse.

I'd like to address one more thing before leaving this topic. There are cases of both. There are split cases which require a different kind of decision making process. In some situations an industry doesn't dissolve, but it dramatically changes. I had a close friend who was a realtor during the real estate crisis in the early 1980's. He decided he wasn't cut out to be a great realtor in a tough market. He switched to mortgage lending and became one of the top producers, who eventually flew all over the country training others in this industry.

Sometimes an industry will shift in one region and continue strong in another. In other words you may be riding a dead horse in California but only be experiencing a dip in Alabama. This may require a decision on relocating or repackaging your natural gifts with new skills and knowledge for a new industry that is growing.

"If you are driven to criticize and find fault with everything that crosses your path, find a way to get paid for it. If you are enthusiastic and expressive, choose a career where these traits are needed and appreciated. Swim with the stream, not against it."

~Nicholas Lore, Founder of the *Rockport Institute*

CHAPTER 18
Disguises

In the early 1930s, the government in Bangkok, Thailand decided to construct a large highway through a village. In our country we would call this exercising the laws of imminent domain. Exercising this law can be extremely controversial here and Thailand was no different. The highway was planned right smack dab through the middle of a Buddhist Monastery. The plan involved relocating the monastery which had a little chapel in the middle. In that chapel was a statue of a very heavy, 11 foot tall clay Buddha.

The government workers used a crane to move the monastery in small pieces. As it worked out, there ended up being a lot more pieces than they had planned. When the workers began to set the Buddha statue in place at the new location, the clay began to crumble and fall apart. As you can imagine, fear broke out. This was an important religious relic and no one wanted it to be lost. But the more the workers tried to set the statue in place, the more clay fell off.

Then they all got the surprise of their life as something quite unexpected was revealed… The statue was solid gold underneath. Before it was moved, the estimated worth of the statue was around $50,000. Overnight the value became millions.

What's the story here? For me the story is that something extremely valuable is often hidden deep inside. That is so true with our strengths. It is more true with some people than others, and with some kinds of strengths more than others. And many talents come disguised as a disability.

My wife, who has worked in education for over 30 years, told me a story recently about a first grade classroom she had visited. While the teacher was teaching in the front of the room, a little girl named Jessica was at the back in constant motion. She was touching her desk but out of her seat and busting moves that would have made Michael Jackson proud. The teacher only had one rule... she could move any way she pleased as long as she kept one hand on the desk.

Shortly after my wife shared this story with me I came across a similar one in Sir Ken Robinson's wonderful book titled *The Element*. Eight year old Gillian's future was already at risk, at least according to her teachers. Late assignments, poor test results, horrible penmanship, fidgeting, and disrupting other students were a few of the complaints. The school decided she had a learning disorder of sorts and suggested that she might do better in a school for children with "special needs".

All this took place in the 1930s, but if you know anything about today's education system, ADHD (Attention Deficit Hyperactivity Disorder) would have likely been the diagnosis. And truckloads of *Ritalin* or one of its successors would have been the prescribed remedy.

But in Gillian's case, the ADHD epidemic hadn't yet been *invented* by pharmaceutical companies waiting to cash in on families. Gillian's mom dressed her up and carted her off to the psychologist.

As Gillian tells the story to Ken Robinson, she says she was invited into an oak paneled room with leather bound books on the shelves. Standing in the room next to a large desk was an imposing man in a tweed jacket. He took Gillian to the far end of the room and sat her down on a huge leather sofa. Gillian's feet didn't quite touch the floor and the setting made her wary. Nervous about the impression she would make, she sat on her hands so that she wouldn't fidget.

Robinson continues Gillian's story, "The psychologist went back to his desk, and for the next twenty minutes asked her mother about the difficulties she was having and the problems the school said she was causing. While he didn't direct any questions at Gillian, he watched her carefully the entire time. Even at this tender age, she knew that this man would have a significant role in her life. She knew what it meant to attend a special school and she didn't want anything to do with that. She genuinely didn't feel she had any real problems, but everyone else seemed to believe she did. Given the way her mother answered the questions, it was possible that even she felt this way.

Maybe, Gillian thought, they were right.

Eventually, Gillian's mother and the psychologist stopped talking. The man rose from his desk, walked to the sofa, and sat next to the little girl. 'Gillian, you've been very patient, and I thank you for that,' he said. 'But I'm afraid you'll have to be patient for a while longer. I need to speak to your mother privately now. We're going to go out of the room for a few minutes. Don't worry we won't be very long.'

Gillian nodded apprehensively, and the two adults left her sitting there on her own. But as he was leaving the room, the psychologist leaned across the desk and turned on the radio.

As soon as they were in the corridor outside the room, the doctor said to Gillian's mother, 'Just wait here for a moment, and watch what she does.' There was a window into the room, and they stood just out of sight. Immediately, Gillian was on her feet, moving around the room to the music. The two adults stood watching quietly for a few minutes, transfixed by the girl's grace. Anyone would have noticed there was something natural – even primal – about Gillian's movements. Just as they would have surely caught the expression of utter pleasure on her face.

At last, the psychologist turned to Gillian's mother and said, 'You know, Mrs. Lynne, Gillian isn't sick. She's a dancer. Take her to dance school.'"
Robinson asked Gillian what happened then. She said, "My mother did exactly what the psychologist suggested. I can't tell you how wonderful it was. I walked into this room, and it was full of people like me. People who couldn't sit still. *People who had to move to think*."

She started going to dance school every week and she practiced at home every day. Eventually, she auditioned for the *Royal Ballet School* in London and was accepted. She went on to join the *Royal Ballet Academy* itself, becoming a soloist and performing all over the world. When that part of her career ended, she formed her own musical theater company and produced a series of highly successful shows in London and New York. Later she met Andrew Lloyd Webber and created with him some of the most successful musical theater productions in history, including *Cats* and *Phantom of the Opera.*

Little Gillian, the girl with the high-risk future, became known to the world as Gillian Lynne, one of the most accomplished choreographers of our time, someone who has brought pleasure to millions and earned millions of dollars. This happened because someone looked deep into her eyes – someone who had seen children like her before and knew how to read the signs. Someone else might have put her on medication and told her to calm down. But Gillian wasn't a problem child. She didn't need to go away to a special school.

She just needed to be who she really was.

According to my wife, our youngest son Justin fit a bit into this wiggly category. When a school official hinted that a drug might help him out, his father Reid wisely responded, "Over my dead body". When my wife tells me this story, I literally get chills... I want to stand up and applaud. Reid intuitively knew that Justin just needed to be who he really was.

My favorite theological professor of all time is a crusty old guy by the name of Howard Hendricks. Howard used to occasionally go out and speak to churches and sometimes he would admonish the Sunday School teachers in the audience, "God tells these kids to wiggle, and you tell them to stop wiggling." How right on he was. And today we put our kids on drugs for our own convenience and refuse to take the time to understand how God wired them in the first place. I'm not saying that there are no kids that could benefit from medication, it's just overdone.

In the May 2011 *Wall Street Journal Magazine*, Richard Branson's mother told interviewer Joshua Levine, "Let's say he was unusual at school. We didn't know if he was 99% stupid and 1% rather exceptional. So we hung on to that 1%."

We know today that billionaire Branson is dyslexic. He has also founded over 400 successful companies, most of them under the name *The Virgin Group – Virgin Records, Virgin Atlantic Airways, Virgin Mobile* and so forth. In the May 13, 2002 issue of *Fortune Magazine* we learn just how disadvantaged Richard is. "He never made it through high school. He has a very poor memory and has a mind that just goes blank at the most inconvenient times. In order to remember, he writes names and other important things on the back of his hand. He won't use a computer. He's terrible at math. Until recently he confesses, he was still confusing gross profit with net profit. He'd been faking it but not too well."

"How much faith you have in the fact that you do carry something special on the inside... that's waiting to get out. Many give up, not knowing they were only 10 minutes from triumph."

~Penny Marshall, Actress, Director, Producer

CHAPTER 19
Dormancy and Delays

Some of our talents and strengths lay dormant due to an inhospitable environment. In 1972 I rode out of Fresno early one Sunday morning headed for Death Valley with a group of cyclists. I was a 9th grader with two friends on the ride, but most were well-conditioned college athletes. In fact most were wrestlers, arguably the best conditioned of all.

About all I can say is, I made it. We rode over Greenhorn pass climbing almost 7,000 feet in a single day. The next day we faced 40 mile an hour head winds for the entire ride. Riding into Death Valley, I don't recall a single flower.

But that doesn't mean Death Valley has no flower potential. In the winter of 2004-2005 something amazing happened. Over seven inches of rain fell in Death Valley, an area with an average rainfall of 2.36 inches. Then in the spring of 2005 something even more amazing happened. Flowers covered the entire Death Valley area. Tourists, botanists and photographers came from all over the world to see it.

As it turns out, Death Valley isn't dead at all. It is laden with potential. It slumbers, just waiting for the right conditions to explode with color and beauty. People are no different.

Sharon Birkman writes, "You don't plant a Ficus where a cactus is going to grow and then expect it to thrive." And Mike Murdock echoes,

"Pineapples do well in Hawaii. They do not do well in Alaska. Atmosphere matters." And in his terrific book, *Why You Can't Be Anything You Want To Be*, Arthur Miller writes, Every person requires particular conditions for their giftedness to thrive."

I've followed professional sports teams all of my life. One thing I've noticed is what I call the Ernie Banks effect. Banks was a shortstop and then a first baseman for the *Chicago Cubs* between 1953 and 1971. Known as Mr. Sunshine and Mr. Cub, he never played in a *World Series*. Although he was an All-Star year in and year out, the Cubs just weren't a very good team during those years. From a *World Series* perspective, Banks' talents stayed dormant.

In football, Joe Montana was a great player. He won four *Super Bowl* rings as the starting quarterback for the *San Francisco 49ers*. A big part of Montana's greatness lay in the fact that he played for a coach (Bill Walsh) and in a system that was perfectly designed for his talents. He was cut out for the short-passing game strategy the *49ers* executed during those years.

Tom Brady's five *Super Bowl* rings are similarly a result of playing in the Bill Belichick system on the *New England Patriots*. Neither Montana nor Brady would have had the success they've enjoyed had they played for other teams.

Michael Jordan and Kobe Bryant were great basketball players. But they were both fortunate to play for Phil Jackson, in systems that magnified their tremendous talents. The same is true of Stephen Curry and the Golden State Warriors today.

In my classes, I always talk about the absence of soccer growing up in a middle class neighborhood. Chances are we had wonderfully talented soccer players, but we didn't play it on our street. The soccer talent was dormant on Michigan Ave.

Today soccer thrives in Fresno, California. You can't drive into a neighborhood without seeing kids playing the game. As of 2018, talent for another game lies dormant. I've yet to see young children playing Cricket, a sport somewhat like baseball and regularly played in the United Kingdom.

Chances are you have some talents that lay completely dormant or aren't being utilized fully. Try placing yourself in different environments that offer new opportunities to try things. Who knows what will grow?

Delays and Late Bloomers

Colonel Sanders was 62 when his *Kentucky Fried Chicken* idea began to take off. He held numerous jobs early in life and just couldn't seem to find his niche. He worked as a steam engine stoker, life insurance salesman and filling station attendant. During the *Great Depression* he began developing his secret recipe with the now famous 11 herbs and spices.

Leonardo didn't paint the Mona Lisa until age 52. God's delays are not God's denials! Sometimes you just need to keep moving forward. Most times you need to keep moving forward while looking for more effective strategies and pathways.

Warren Buffett was a full-time investor in the stock market before he made his first million. As Keith Cunningham says, "I don't know anyone who would read a book or sign up for a course title, 'How to Make $1,000,000 in Only 9 Years.'"

Our culture has taught us that success should be instant, radical and easy. The reality is that success is usually slow, methodical and somewhat difficult, even when working from your strengths.

Late Blooming Bulls

Dennis was an insecure little boy. He was the family runt, short, awkward and struggled to sink a layup. He warmed the bench for a half season of high school basketball and then quit. He was 5'9" when he graduated, and endured taunting by his friends when he tagged along with his bigger, younger, more athletic sisters.

After graduation, Dennis took a job on the graveyard shift sweeping floors at the *Dallas/Fort Worth International Airport.* One night, he stuck a broom through the safety gate of a shuttered airport gift shop and fished out a few dozen watches that he distributed among his friends. He got caught. Dennis didn't last long in that job. But his something big had already started to happen. In the two years since high school, Dennis had grown like kelp. He was working part-time scrubbing cars at an Oldsmobile dealership for $3.50 an hour when he topped out at 6'8".

So Dennis started to play basketball and found that he was suddenly less gawky despite being taller and more muscular. He caught on to the game so quickly it was as if the basketball fairy had left hoop skills under his pillow one night. In his words, "It was like I had a new body that knew how to do all this stuff the old one didn't."

A family friend convinced Dennis to try out for a local community college team. He played for a while, but dropped out with academic problems. The following year, 1983, he accepted a basketball scholarship to *South-Western Oklahoma State*, a little known *NAIA* school. He dominated there for three years, averaging 25.7 points and an otherworldly 15.7 rebounds per game.

The rest is hardwood history. Dennis Rodman was drafted into the *NBA* and in fourteen years won five championships, was twice named Defensive Player of the Year, and became the greatest rebounder in *NBA* history. In 2011, the man who played hardly any organized basketball before he was twenty-one, was inducted into the *Basketball Hall of Fame*.

Scottie was 6'1" when he graduated from high school. He started college, not as a player, but a team manager - the guy that takes care of the equipment. But something happened while he was the team manager at the little known *University of Central Arkansas*. He grew to 6'3" by the end of his first year and started playing for the team. By the end of the following summer, Scottie was 6'5". By his junior season he was 6'7" and *NBA* scouts began to swarm the stands to watch unheralded *Central Arkansas*. Scottie Pippen ended up playing for the *Chicago Bulls* and by the end of his career was named one of the fifty greatest players in *NBA* history and was inducted into the *Basketball Hall of Fame*.

"Parts are aspects or qualities of a person: the efficient part, the stay-at-home part, the nurturing part, the shopper part, the baby, the glamor girl and all the other selves and facets that make up the whole individual."

~Anne Linden

CHAPTER 20
Dynamic Tension

All of us have had the experience of conflicting parts…. Part of me wants to do this, part of me wants to do something else. Part of me wants pizza, part of me wants to go for Chinese. Part of me wants to exercise, part of me wants to lie down and veg. And for most of us, the parts conflict will at some point extend to our career life.

Tim Butler is the Director of Career Development at *Harvard Business School* and the author of *Getting Unstuck: How Dead Ends Become New Paths.* In the book, Butler talks about the phenomenon he refers to as impasse. Impasse just means you are stuck, that in some way you can't move forward. Often this is because there is a part of you that wants to be expressed or wants to be expressed more fully. It may come out as "something missing" or "things just aren't working" or a "deadness at work".

Butler is clear that impasse is a very normal part of career development. It doesn't mean you've blown a career decision, gone to work for the wrong company or taken the wrong job. It does mean that you need to be looking for ways and places where your talents and energies can be expressed more fully. This may or may not mean a different company, job or career choice.

The 100 Jobs Exercise is one way Butler exposes the parts conflict, pulling out themes and images that he refers to as "Dynamic Tensions".

I've taken Butler's concept and modified it to dovetail with the *ONET* System. The synchronization with *ONET* Jobs will allow you to do fairly deep research into the actual day-to-day tasks. Beyond that, the *100 Jobs Exercise* tool is also a way to elicit deep images and aspects of yourself that are not being currently expressed sufficiently in your current life or work situation. In other words, it's a way to identify passion, talents and values that aren't being realized. Again, it's an incredibly useful tool to identify your "Dynamic Tensions".

Go through the list of 100 jobs on the next page. Quickly go through the list and place a check mark next to any career that interests you for any reason. Then go back through the list and narrow down your initial choices. Circle the 10 careers that are most appealing.

While this may give you some ideas of a future career direction or re-direction, the purpose at this point is only to identify dynamic tensions or parts conflict.

If for example, you select Military Officer, Homemaker and Surgeon in this exercise, you have some dynamic tensions that will need to be integrated. There are any number of tension possibilities. Maybe you have both a desire to "manage people" and you also have a desire to "make strong individual contributions". Or you could have a desire to "work alone" and a desire to "be the one in charge". Again, the number of possible dynamic tensions is almost endless.

Make some notes on any conflicts that jump out at you.

Top Ten Careers	**Tensions**

112

Accountant	Financial Analyst	Political Science Professor
Admin Services Manager	Fine Artist (Paint, Sculpt)	Police Officer
Advertising Copywriter	Firefighter	Post Office Service Clerk
Advertising Sales Agent	Food Service Manager	Professional Athlete
Arbitrator-Mediator	Foreign Language Translator	Program Director Radio/TV
Architect	Fundraiser	Proofreader
Automobile Mechanic	Graphic Designer	Public Relations Specialist
Bank Branch Manager	High School Teacher	Quality Control Analyst
Bookkeeper	Home Economics Teacher	Real Estate Salesperson
Broadcast News Analyst	Homemaker	Registered Nurse
Carpenter	Human Resources Manager	Research Scientist
Chief Executive	Industrial Production Mgr	Retail Salesperson
Child-Care Worker	Investigative Reporter	Retail Store Manager
City Planner	Investment Fund Manager	Secretary Admin. Assistant
Civil Engineer	Legislator	Senior Military Leader
Computer System Manager	Librarian	Set Exhibit Designer
Computer Systems Analyst	Lodging and Hotel Manager	Ship Captain
Computer User Support	Logistical Planner	Social Service Manager
Counseling Psychologist	Management Analyst	Social Worker
Courtroom Lawyer	Manufacturing Engineer	Sociologist
Creative Writer	Marketing Manager	Software Designer
Credit Counselor	Marketing Researcher	Solar Thermal Tech Installer
Data Entry	Mathematician	Speech Pathologist
Director Religious Activities	Medical Health Service Mgr	Sports Coach
Director, Stage, Film, TV	Medical Scientist	Sports Official
Economist	Meeting Event Planner	Statistician
Education Administrator	Military Serviceperson	Stockbroker Securities Sales
Education Teacher	Museum Conservator	Surgeon
Electrical Engineer	Music Composer Arranger	Technical Product Sales
Electrician	Newspaper Editor	Theoretical Physicist
Emergency Medical Tech	Operations Manager	Treasurer Controller
Entertainer (Actor, Singer)	Optometrist	Veterinarian
Farm and Ranch Manager	Personal Financial Advisor	Video Game Designer
File Clerk	Philosophy Teacher	

Finding Your Mash Up

How do you deal with dynamic tensions? You have to integrate them. Road Trip Nation co-creator Nathan Gebhard talks about combining interests and passions. When doing high school presentations, he asks the students in the audience what they are interested in? He asks them to combine interests like art and writing, sports and science and then come up with an occupation. At one presentation, a student said, "I like walking and turtles. I want to be a turtle walker." So as part of the presentation, Nathan played a video, and behind the scenes had the staff *Google* "Turtle Walking". They literally found a woman who worked at a rehabilitation center for turtles. Within minutes they had the student up on stage, on the phone talking to a real-life turtle walker.

Growing up in the 1950's, Ed had two boyhood idols, Walt Disney and Albert Einstein. As he explains it, "Disney was all about inventing the new and Einstein was about explaining that which already was". Ed decided he wanted to be a Disney animator and pursued it. But it became clear his drawing wasn't good enough and the pathway to get there wasn't very well laid out. Ed decided to pursue his other love, science. He graduated with two degrees, one in physics and the other in a then emerging field called computer science. Ed met a man who encouraged him to pursue an even more obscure subset of computer science. It was called computer graphics. All of a sudden, the other childhood dream was back in play. At age 26, Ed set a goal to develop a way to animate, not with pencil and paper, but using a computer. In 1972, he made his first short animated film. In 1986, he became the president of a new hardware company called Pixar Image Computer. Ed Catmull went on to co- found Pixar Animation collaborating with people like Steve Jobs and John Lassiter.

I will discuss this a little more in Chapter 31 on "Parts".

"I very much believe in things unseen, both of positive and destructive energy. I absolutely believe in spiritual warfare and have experienced it in my life."

~Ashley Judd

Chapter 21
Disempowering Forces

If you are a *Stranger Things* fan maybe this chapter will be of interest to you. If you are a scientific type that doesn't believe in the supernatural, feel free to skip it. But it's good to remember that even scientists believe in things they can't see. Atoms, Quarks, Leptons, Bosons, Preons, Strings, Black Holes and Energy all refer to things most of us believe in, yet don't see. Yet we do see the results. And its those results that move us to believing that they do indeed exist. Most of us, at some level would agree that evil exists in the world. Do we see it? Or do we believe it because of the results?

The English poet-painter William Blake (1757-1827) achieved almost no recognition during his lifetime. His paintings and poetry have been characterized as part of the *Romantic Period* and today are considered some of the greatest works of art ever produced.

Blake claimed that he always had a voice inside telling him that he was wasting his life, that his art was useless and that he was a man who was barely able to support his family. Blake said the voice would grow louder every time he was about to begin a new project that was full of possibility but also the chance of failure. Tired of this persistent voice, he gave it a name so that he could better recognize it and better deal with its attacks. Blake called it the "accuser", based on terminology from the Jewish-Christian Scriptures. Taken from the original Hebrew, this is the core meaning of the word for satan. The second part of the Bible known as the New Testament was originally written in Greek. There the word diabolos was used. It means, "one who speaks against".

Harvard Business School Director of Career Development Timothy Butler was mentioned in a previous chapter as the developer of the *100 Jobs Exercise*. In chapter two of his book, *Getting Stuck*, Butler expounds on this phenomena as it relates to what he calls career impasse, "The accuser is the voice that tells us we have failed, that we are inadequate, that we have made wrong choices, that we are unworthy, or that we are not attractive enough. This accuser says that our energy for innovation and our readiness for change are impulses not to be trusted. It is the loudest voice within us, and its concern is not to redress wrongs or take moral action; its concern is to punish and stop us from taking that action which would allow us to experience new possibilities."

Butler continues, "The inner critic can be crippling. We must learn to recognize this enemy, for recognition is the first step in preventing this adversary from stopping us. Each of us has an accuser with a particular personality and a specific way of delivering a disheartening message. If we do not recognize the accuser, then our feelings of guilt, shame or inadequacy are vague and undifferentiated. They become merely who we are rather than the voice of an unhelpful intruder."

Richard Carson has written an interesting book titled, *Taming Your Gremlin*. It was a significant piece of the training I received at the *Coaches Training Institute* in 1999. The book reads, "Your gremlin is the narrator in your head. He tells you who and how you are, and he defines and interprets your every experience. Your gremlin is not your negative thoughts – he is the source of them. He is not your less-than-positive past experiences – he uses them. He is not your fears – he taunts you with them by creating the horror movie about your future that you sometimes watch."

I have no idea what kind of spiritual beliefs either Butler or Richard Carson hold. I come from a perspective that is uniquely my own, but consistently informed by the Jewish-Christian Scriptures. I am a follower of Jesus, imperfect and hopefully growing every day. From where I sit, there exists an invisible dimension, a spirit realm that each of us lives in. From my own experience and others I know very well, these descriptions are accurate, they literally exist and are clearly identified in Scripture. While we all have "Parts", unique aspects within our personality described in the last chapter as dynamic tensions, these accusers are conveying something completely different. In the first century, a Jesus follower by the name of Paul wrote, "We are not fighting against flesh-and-blood enemies, but against evil rulers and authorities of the unseen world, against mighty powers in this dark world, and against evil spirits."

This is a career book and the subject goes a bit beyond intended purposes. That being said, if your career is stuck, consider there is a spiritual component to the issues. I'm convinced there is a Creator-God that designed you for a very specific assignment on this planet. I'm also convinced that He placed within you passion and talents, that if followed, will lead you into that assignment.

If that's true, consider that there are enemies trying to keep you from discovering your assignment. And if you do discover it, they will work even harder to keep you from fulfilling it. These accusing voices that Butler and Carson speak of is their go-to strategy. They will do anything they can to keep you living discouraged and defeated.

William Blake believed that identification was the critical step. Write down the images and phrases your own accuser brings against you. They are predictable and often begin with words like:

You should have _____.
You are too _____.
You should be more _____.

Then pay attention to where you feel the accusations in your body. Do your shoulders slouch? Is there a queasy feeling in the pit of your stomach? Is there a tightness in your chest? Do you feel weak? For many, they show up as nightmares or night terrors.

119

Motivational speaker Lance Wallnau asks the question, "How do you know you're under attack?" Wallnau says, "One of the things I've noticed is that when I'm in warfare I don't feel like myself. I feel disconnected, awkward and inauthentic. I'm not myself and I don't even like who is showing up. It's like you're someone else. Something is trying to take over your thought process."

Wallnau continues talking about the Scriptural concept of a stronghold, "What is a stronghold? Think of it as a house made of thoughts. It's a pattern of thinking that has a 'strong hold' grip on your mind. A stronghold is something that exerts an influence or leverage over the thought patterns that play in your mind. Strongholds are like fortresses that need to be torn down one brick at a time. Every thought that hits you needs to be countered with another thought! Lies need to be answered with the truth. These truths need to be meditated upon and literally engrafted into your soul."

I got some good Bible-based counseling and learned to manage these mind-monsters. You might want to consider the same.

The Scripture talks about "casting down" destructive thoughts and imaginings. Bible teacher Joyce Meyer has a number of resources that you might find helpful. Her book titled, *Battlefield of the Mind* is a terrific resource. Lance Wallnau has several resources. One of my favorites is *Doing Business Supernaturally*.

If these ideas stretch you beyond what you're comfortable with, I get it. It took me a long time to recognize the reality of these concepts. Think about it. This could be the big breakthrough you've been looking for!

Section III

The STRENGTHSPATH

SOLUTION

The first sections of this book were devoted to helping you understand some of the problems you have faced in selecting a career that fits. If I were to summarize the problem with most careers, it is disengaged strengths.

This next section deals with solutions to those problems. If the primary problem is disengaged strengths, it stands to reason that the solution might be to engage your strengths. I'll share eight of the most important strengths to explore and then share a few practical ways to engage, embed and execute them.

The first part of the solution is to identify or discover your strengths. Once we have engaged in the process of discovery and have clearly and accurately identified some of our strengths, we can begin to develop or polish them. We also need to learn how to describe, display and demonstrated our strengths so that others become aware of the ways we add value. And the bottom line is delivery. The purpose of our strengths are to add value, serve and contribute to others.

"Passion Matters. When we're focused on and operating in our strengths and passions, nothing can hold us back…. When you love what you do you will work like crazy – but it will never feel like work."

~Dave Ramsey

Chapter 22
Passion

You will never maximize your career or become the best version of yourself until you are spending most of your work hours on something that excites you. You can only operate from pure discipline for so long, and then it's exhausting. When you love what you do, you will jump out of bed every morning and will be excited to get to work. And as a result, you will maximize your success. Passion will automatically drive you to work smarter, harder and longer. You will endure failures with comeback after comeback. And that's a great way to invest your life.

Passion is a huge success multiplier. It creates energy and attracts sales like a magnet. In short, passionate people are more successful because they care more than dispassionate people. Passionate people care more than the average entrepreneur or employee. If they care more than you, chances are they will be more successful.

This component might also be referred to as a natural affinity, appetite, strong interest or desire. Your passion is a topic or task you are drawn to. It's an activity or subject area that makes you feel strong.

Harvard University career services director, Dr. Timothy Butler refers to passion as, "Deeply Embedded Life Interests". Butler writes, "Think of a deeply embedded life interest as a geothermal pool of superheated water.

It will rise to the surface in one place as a hot spring and in another as a geyser. But beneath the surface—at the core of the individual—the pool is constantly bubbling. Deeply embedded life interests always seem to find expression, even if a person has to change jobs—or careers—for that to happen. Mature adults have particular patterns of lifelong passions that remain stable over long periods."

Butler also uses the phrases, *Deep Interest Pattern* and *Deep Structure Interests.* Butler offers more on this topic, "Each of us has a unique pattern of interests, a 'potential self' that seeks expression. One of the most interesting findings in career psychology research is that underlying patterns of work interest are a relatively enduring feature of a person."

Butler continues, "There is evidence that, amid this stability, new experiences in work environments continue to influence the development of interests, but *within the contours of the deep interest pattern.* Deep structure interests are one of the most basic features of an individual. They are deeply rooted and enduring, and they naturally push to find an avenue of expression."

Butler offers Andy Warhol's deep structure creativity interest as an example. Warhol's creativity was realized through his work in advertising, paintings and films. Similarly Richard Feynman's deep structure interest is seen in his scientific research, his writings and his lectures. Butler contends that any work that is not adequately grounded in a person's deep structure interests will not last. Albert Einstein might have become a mathematician or a chemist instead of a physicist, but he would never have succeeded as a military officer. Bill Gates would never have succeeded as a food services manager. This is not because either Einstein or Gates had a poor attitude.

I heard Oprah Winfrey share this insight, "Every single person who is super successful always says in some form that following your bliss or **following your passion is the way for you to be the most successful** and empowered person." *Facebook* Chief Operating Officer Sheryl

Sandberg says, "You will not be as successful as you could be if you only like what you do and don't love it." After forty years of studying human potential, I have to agree.

This does not mean that success is not hard. Steve Jobs told us that it is exactly because success is so very hard that we need to discover our passion. Historically, passion incorporated the idea of suffering. What is it that you love to do so much that you are willing to suffer for it?

I don't believe you will ever maximize your career or become the best version of yourself until you are spending most of your work hours on something that excites you. You can only operate from pure discipline for so long, and then it's exhausting. When you love what you do, you will jump out of bed every morning and will be excited to get to work. And as a result, you will maximize your success. Passion will automatically drive you to work smarter, harder and longer. You will endure failures with comeback after comeback. And that's a great way to spend your time at work.

For some, passion discovery is elusive. Sometimes this is fear, disguised as practicality. Following your passion can be a radical act that must overcome pressure from public opinion, parents, partners, professors and promoters. But the discovery process is worth it. Think about these words of Dr. Wayne Dyer, "There's no scarcity of opportunity to make a living at what you love. There is only a scarcity of resolve to make it happen."

"Your talents are worth your devotion. Stop saying you don't have time or it might not make money. Your talents are another form of oxygen you need to breathe in this lifetime."

~Tama J. Kieves

CHAPTER 23
Potential

Your Potential is your Talent. Similar concepts are aptitude, inborn ability, gifting, knack, flair, bent, instinct, genius, inclination, brilliance and forte. Potential is what you can be good at. And to paraphrase Lady Gaga, *Baby They Were Born This Way*. Talents are innate and enduring.

Larry Winget is one motivator that finally tells it like it is, "You can do whatever you want to do. **Wrong**. You can do whatever you have the talent to do. And you have more talent to do more things than you have given yourself credit for up until now."

The late *Gallup* leader Don O. Clifton writes, "Talents naturally occur within you and cannot be acquired. They are inborn predispositions. They are things that you do instinctively." And Marcus Buckingham adds, "Talent is a naturally recurring pattern of thought, feeling, or behavior that can be productively applied."

In her book *Multipliers,* Liz Wiseman explains, "A native genius is something that people do, not only exceptionally well, but absolutely naturally. They do it easily (without extra effort) and freely (without condition). What people do easily, they do without conscious effort. They do it better than anything else they do, but they don't need to apply extraordinary effort to the task. It is effortless, and they stand ready and willing to contribute, whether it is a formal job requirement or not. Finding someone's native genius is the key that unlocks discretionary effort. It propels people to go beyond what is required and offer their full intelligence. Finding people's genius begins by carefully observing them in action, looking for spikes of authentic enthusiasm and a natural flow of energy."

These talents give each person a special ability to do certain kinds of tasks easily and happily, yet also make other tasks seem like pure torture. Can you imagine comedian Robin Williams trying to work as an accountant?

Talents are inborn or innate. Talents are instinctual. Talents are natural. When an employee uses a talent, they might experience what I call a **"made for this moment"**. They might get a sense that they were made or born to do that activity.

Using talents, like breathing, may seem almost effortless. At least it feels easy. That doesn't mean a worker doesn't need to work hard at building on their talent, but it might feel like they're not working as hard.

Talents often show up early in life although there is frequently not an adult around who is paying attention.

Rapid learning is a strong sign of talent. Results or success are a sign of talent. By learning how to hire for talent, instead of just skills, your training costs will drop and your employee will succeed bigger and faster. As The Container Store founder Kip Tindell says, "One Great Employee = Three Good Employees." Discovering talent will help you hire that "One Great Employee".

Dilbert is a very successful comic strip written by Scott Adams. He regularly lampoons what's ridiculous about corporate America. A few years back, a TV cartoon series was developed based on the Dilbert character. There is a great clip from one of the episodes circulating on YouTube that perfectly gives an example of what I'm talking about when I use the term "talent path". In the clip, Dilbert's mom takes him to the doctor with a concern about his habit of tearing mechanical devices apart around the house. He had just disassembled the television, a clock and a stereo and then used the components to build a ham radio set. (I hear stories like this all the time in my classes.)

The doctor shares with Dilbert's mom that he has a rare condition called *"The Knack"*. "The Knack," continues the doctor, "is a rare condition characterized by all things mechanical and electrical... and utter social ineptitude. He won't be able to lead a normal life... in fact he will be forced to become an engineer."

I'm convinced that every applicant that comes into your system has "The Knack" although it may have absolutely nothing to do with mechanical aptitudes. Their "Knack" may be with music, marketing, ministry or any one of 10,000 other things.

Generically their knack will include *Aptitude* Talents, *Activity* Talents and *Approach* Talents forming what I call the Talent Triangle.

Aptitudes

Aptitudes are potential and they are underlying drivers of unique ability. I believe they are connected with individualized areas of intelligence. *Harvard* professor, Howard Gardner has done extensive research with Savants, those with brain injuries and people who have succeeded wildly, but often in very narrow niches. He concludes that there are ability specific regions of the brain, and therefore multiple intelligences or aptitudes in up to nine areas. He suggests that most people have not one intelligence or set of aptitudes but a unique blend or hierarchy of several including:

Word Aptitudes
Number/Logic Aptitudes
Picture Aptitudes
Music Aptitudes
Body Aptitudes
People Aptitudes
Self Awareness Aptitudes
*This lists Gardner's original seven

Gardner says we should not be asking, "How smart is this individual?" Rather we should be asking, "How is this individual smart?"

The *Johnson O'Connor Foundation* grew out of aptitude and job fit research at *General Electric*. For career selection assessments, it may be one of the most helpful. They use work sample tests, which tend to be the most accurate. However, they no longer conduct pre-employment assessments.

Johnson O'Connor accesses for 19 or 20 aptitudes including:

Personality – Preference for working in groups or alone
Graphoria – Clerical ability with figures and symbols
Ideaphoria – Fluency of ideas
Structural Visualization* – Ability to think in 3 dimensions
Abstract Visualization – Ability to work with ideas
Inductive Reasoning – See connections in scattered facts
Analytical Reasoning – Separating into component parts
Finger Dexterity – Manipulating fingers skillfully
Tweezer Dexterity - Handling small tools easily
Observation – Taking careful notice
Design Memory – Memorizing designs rapidly
Tonal Memory – Remembering sounds and music notes
Pitch Discrimination – Differentiate musical tones
Rhythmic Ability – Ability to keep time
Timbre Discrimination – Detect sounds of same pitch & volume
Number Memory – Remembering numbers of all kinds
Proportional Appraisal – Discerning harmonious designs
Silograms – Ability to learn languages and technical jargon
Foresight – Look into the future with wisdom
Color Perception – Distinguish colors

The *Johnson O'Connor Laboratory* has also measured eye dominance, physical energy, taste for sour and vocabulary.

*The *Foundation* no longer includes Abstract Visualization in its results. In the early years it wasn't tested for directly but measured as an inverse quality opposite to structural visualization.

O*NET – Abilities

Abilities - Enduring attributes of the individual that influence performance.

O*NET (Occupational Information Network) is a website run by the Department of Labor. It has a lot of good information that can help both candidates and companies better understand aptitudes, activities and how they connect with different work roles. The Handbook of Human Abilities – Definitions, Measurements and Job Task Requirements, written by Edwin A. Fleishman and Maureen E. Reilly is one of the main source documents for much of the information. The website has short definitions of each ability listed below. To see these along with definitions of each go to the O*NET website: https://www.onetonline.org/find/descriptor/browse/Abilities/

Cognitive	Physical	Psychomotor	Sensory
Category Flexibility	Dynamic Flexibility	Arm-Hand Steadiness	Auditory Attention
Deductive Reasoning	Dynamic Strength	Control Precision	Depth Perception
Flexibility of Closure	Explosive Strength	Finger Dexterity	Far Vision
Fluency of Ideas	Extent Flexibility	Manual Dexterity	Glare Sensitivity
Inductive Reasoning	Gross Body Coord.	Multi-Limb Coordination	Hearing Sensitivity
Information Ordering	Gross Body Equilib.	Rate Control	Near Vision
Mathematical Reasoning	Stamina	Reaction Time	Night Vision
Memorization	Static Strength	Response Orientation	Peripheral Vision
Number Facility	Trunk Strength	Speed of Limb Movement	Sound Location
Oral Comprehension		Wrist-Finder Speed	Speech Clarity
Originality			Speech Recognition
Perceptual Speed			Color Discrimination
Problem Sensitivity			
Selective Attention			
Spatial Orientation			
Speed of Closure			
Time Sharing			
Visualization			
Written Comprehension			
Written Expression			

Most of us will benefit from simply studying the definitions of these abilities and the types of work that connect with them. Just reading through the list of abilities with their accompanying definitions and descriptions will provide a few aha moments.

Activities

Based on your Aptitudes, you have varying degrees of potential to perform well in different kinds of activities. **Activity Talents** will often fall into **Four Types** or often a combination of type preferences.

The four include:

Working with People

Advise, Analyze, Build, Coach, Coordinate, Develop, Direct, Evaluate, Help, Inform, Inspire, Interview, Lead, Manage, Motivate, Observe, Organize, Persuade, Recruit, Rehabilitate, Research, Select, Serve, Sketch, Supervise, Teach, Test, Train, Unite

Working with Things

Adapt, Analyze, Arrange, Assemble, Balance, Budget, Build, Classify, Clean, Collect, Cook, Create, Deliver, Design, Diagnose, Display, Distribute, Drive, Estimate, Examine, Fix, Grow, Imagine, Improve, Inspect, Install, Invent, Inventory, Maintain, Operate, Paint, Photograph, Promote, Restore, Select, Sell, Sew, Set Up, Show, Sketch, Test, Weigh

Working with Ideas

Analyze, Arrange, Assemble, Brainstorm, Classify, Collect, Communicate, Connect, Create, Describe, Design, Develop, Discover, Display, Dramatize, Edit, Expand, Experiment, Express, File, Fix, Illustrate, Imagine, Implement, Improve, Improvise, Manage, Promote, Question, Recommend, Research, Sell, Shape, Share, Study, Summarize, Synergize, Systemize, Teach, Test

Working with Data or Information

Analyze, Arrange, Classify, Check, Collect, Communicate, Consolidate, Discover, Dissect, Edit, Explain, File, Illustrate, Interpret, Investigate, Log, Manage, Memorize, Organize, Protect, Question, Read, Research, Restore, Retrieve, Sell, Sort, Study, Summarize, Synthesize, Systemize, Test, Transcribe, Understand

That's a start, but you'll want to get even more granular in your self-awareness and which activities you have the most potential to excel in.

Approaches

To explain the difference between Approaches, Activities and Aptitudes, let's consider comedians and crime fighters. First let's imagine you're hiring a comedian.

The job of a comedian or comic is to make people laugh. That is a talent or aptitude. But there are many approaches to that talent. Some of the approaches are related to a particular medium, but even within a single medium, there are many approaches.

You may make people laugh as a comedic actor, a comedy writer, a comic strip creator or a stand-up comedian. As a comic strip creator, you may have the gift for a single panel or multi-panel strip. You might have the ability to do both, but it's likely you'll be better at one or the other. And then consider the content and style of the strip. Could *Peanuts* creator Charles Schultz produce in the style of *Far Side* creator Gary Larson? I doubt it. Even within a single medium, their "Approaches" to comic strip humor are vastly different.

Consider "Approaches" to stand-up comedy. My favorite comedians include the quiet, slow talking Steven Wright and the zany maniacal Robin Williams. They both make me laugh. But their approaches to stand-up comedy are worlds apart. Make a list of 10 people that make you laugh. It's the same result, but not one of them will do it exactly the same way. Some are extremely gifted with physical comedy. That is, they use their body. With others, like Jim Carrey, it's facial expressions. Some tell a long story with a device called the "running gag". The late Johnny Carson had a way of getting laughs from his response to his jokes that didn't get laughs. When his topical humor sagged, he got funnier. Jerry Seinfeld's observational humor digs deeply into the minutia of everyday life.

Now imagine you're hiring a crimefighter or superhero? What makes them interesting isn't their crime fighting. What makes them interesting is how they do it. They all fight crime. Essentially they get the same results. The bad guys lose. But they all use a completely unique set of talents or powers. Superman, Batman, Green Hornet, Hulk, Spiderman, Wonder Woman and Thor are all very different in their approach. But each one has discovered, developed and delivers a set of strengths that are unique to them. And so should you. What's your superpower?

Strengthsfinder 2.0

If you would like a terrific assessment to help you identify your "Approach Talents", I recommend *Gallup's Strengthsfinder 2.0* which helps you identify a unique hierarchy of 34 Approaches to any activity. Each of the 34 Approaches is classified under four Types including: **Executing, Influencing, Relationship Building and Strategic Thinking.** *Strengthsfinder 2.0* then gets more detailed or more granular. Each theme has underlying threads that explains the domain.

Executing Type	Influencing Type	Relating Type	Strategic Thinking Type
Achiever	Activator	Adaptability	Analytical
Arranger	Command	Developer	Context
Belief	Communication	Connectedness	Futuristic
Consistency	Competition	Empathy	Ideation
Deliberate	Maximizer	Harmony	Input
Discipline	Self-Assurance	Includer	Intellection
Focus	Significance	Individualization	Learner
Responsibility	Woo	Positivity	Strategic
Restorative		Relator	

O*NET Work Styles

The *Occupational Information Network (O*NET)* provides a similar concept. They describe *Workstyles* as, "Personal characteristics that can affect how well someone performs a job." I would put some of these characteristics in the character category. Some like Initiative, Persistence and Self Control are choices more than traits. But it's still a worthwhile list. And like everything in *O*NET,* each item connects back to over 1100 jobs.

Achievement/Effort — Job requires establishing and maintaining personally challenging achievement goals and exerting effort toward mastering tasks.

Adaptability/Flexibility — Job requires being open to change (positive or negative) and to considerable variety in the workplace.

Analytical Thinking — Job requires analyzing information and using logic to address work-related issues and problems.

Attention to Detail — Job requires being careful about detail and thorough in completing work tasks.

Concern for Others — Job requires being sensitive to others' needs and feelings and being understanding and helpful on the job.

Cooperation — Job requires being pleasant with others on the job and displaying a good-natured, cooperative attitude.

Dependability — Job requires being reliable, responsible, and dependable, and fulfilling obligations.

Independence — Job requires developing one's own ways of doing things, guiding oneself with little or no supervision, and depending on oneself to get things done.

Initiative — Job requires a willingness to take on responsibilities and challenges.

Innovation — Job requires creativity and alternative thinking to develop new ideas for and answers to work-related problems.

Integrity — Job requires being honest and ethical.

Leadership — Job requires a willingness to lead, take charge, and offer opinions and direction.

Persistence — Job requires persistence in the face of obstacles.

Self Control — Job requires maintaining composure, keeping emotions in check, controlling anger, and avoiding aggressive behavior, even in very difficult situations.

Social Orientation— Job requires preferring to work with others rather than alone, and being personally connected with others on the job.

Stress Tolerance — Job requires accepting criticism and dealing calmly and effectively with high stress situations.

"Personality style is the way a person acts when he or she is able to do things his or her own way. Most people are consistent enough in their behavior to allow you to predict their behavior."

~Kate Ward

CHAPTER 24
Personality

The third element of your unique set of strengths is your **PERSONALITY** or temperament. It correlates heavily with the end of the last chapter and what I described as Approach Talents. You might think of your personality style as a kind of map that suggests both the inner geography and the outward direction of your life. Whether you know it or not, to some extent, you follow its path every single day of your life.

We all spend a great deal of time assessing the personalities and temperaments of others. In a basic sense, it is simply getting to know, understand and then describe someone. As soon as we begin to describe a person, we generally use trait, temperament and personality language to do it.

People generally behave in patterned, organized and recognizable ways. If we say that someone is outgoing, we usually mean that they are outgoing with some degree of regularity. A pattern is implied. With some consistency, we can also say that some traits often come packaged together in a somewhat unique, yet similar and discernible grouping that we might call a personality type.

The evidence is strong that our personality comes from at least three places:

Nature – Your temperament is innate and natural from birth. These traits often show up as early as infancy and nearly always as toddlers.

Nurture - It is also influenced or shaped by environment, family, culture and friends.

Choice - Personality is a combined set of behaviors that to some extent can be expressed at will. For example, I am naturally reserved, but I can choose to be gregarious and outgoing when the occasion calls for it. But it doesn't come naturally and I expend a tremendous amount of energy to do it.

Everyone seems to have patterns and natural preferences that can be observed.

Personalities can be described in terms of individual traits. Some personality psychologists explain them as a position on an axis or line between opposites. Examples are:

- Intense or Relaxed?
- Shy or Outgoing?
- Fast or Slow?
- Options-open or Decisive?
- Analytical or Active?
- Independent or Dependent?
- Extroverted or Introverted?
- Leader or Follower?
- Flexible or Structured?

Some of the above traits are inextricably attached to the level of success you will achieve in a given role! Some roles may optimize if you have paradoxical or complimentary traits. It's worth your time to figure out the connections.

Often personality traits show up in groups. Those natural groupings have led to numerous sorting systems.

There are three different personality sorting systems that I have studied and use with clients and all three have applications to hiring. The three systems include:

- *D.I.S.C.*
- *Myers-Briggs* or *16 Type or Style*
- *Meta-Programs* from *Neuro-Linguistic Programming*

Never allow any assessment to define you with a declarative statement. But personality assessments can give you "hints" or "clues" that offer self-discovery insight. To maximize assessment results, make sure you customize the report. Highlight the descriptions that describe you best. In some cases you may have a partner or close friend read over the report and offer feedback. Ask them to re-write any inaccurate description so that it precisely portrays your personality. Realize that everyone can learn to **"play in all the rooms"**. Some rooms will just be more comfortable.

The *D.I.S.C.* Profile

The *DISC* Profile is the most popular assessment used by organizations worldwide. Over 50 million people have used the instrument to communicate better and understand their talents and non-talents. *DISC* first came to prominence in the military - it was widely used as part of the *US Army's* recruitment process during the years leading to the *Second World War*. Having proved its value, it gradually came to be used in a business recruitment setting. Although the history goes all the way back to Hippocrates, around 500 B.C., the modern assessment was first developed by psychologist William Marston who was a very interesting man. He was also the inventor of the lie-detector test and the superhero *Wonder Woman*. Marston never attempted to copyright the assessment, so today, slightly different versions are produced by different vendors.

DISC starts with only four basic behavior types, naturally grouping several dozen traits that commonly show up together.

Each letter in *DISC* represents a different trait grouping. The four types combine into thousands of possible patterns reflecting the complexity of human strengths. Sophisticated reports show up to 28 personality blends.

How I Use *D.I.S.C.*

• Suggest Potential Job Matches
• Identify Job Search Challenges
• Use In Building Interview Strategies
• Training Leaders and Managers

D.I.S.C Style Overview

Direct	Interactive
Direct	Interacting
Directive	Influencing
Doer	Inducing
Determined	Inspiring
Decisive	Initiating
Destination	Inclusive
Daring	Instigating
Dominant	Immediate
Driving	Inviting
Problem Area-Demanding	Problem Area-Impulsive
Conceptual	**Stabilizing**
Conceptual	Stabilizing
Conscientious	Steadying
Cautious	Sincere
Calculating	Supporting
Consistent	Standardizing
Classifying	Sympathetic
Compliant	Social Sameness
Contemplating	Sacrificial
Controlled	Serving
Problem Area-Critical	Problem Area-Slow

It's not a perfect tool. **Everyone has a little of each style**. To get a quick sense of your own special blend, read each of the descriptors in the four categories and assign a number 1-10 (10 meaning it very much describes you) for how much the word describes you.

Myers-Briggs – 16 Type or Style

Another very popular personality model is *Myers-Briggs* or the *16 Type*. The *Myers-Briggs* is more complicated to explain in a short space. It is loosely based on Carl Jung's Psychological Model and Typology that suggests everyone has certain preferences including ways of thinking, perceiving, interacting, behaving and deciding. Typologists believe these preferences are primarily innate traits, similar to left and right handedness. The model sorts these inclinations into four preference pairs that together result in 16 Psychological Types. On this page you'll find the four preferences with lists describing each set of traits. On the following page is an overview of the 16 Psychological Types or Styles that come from the four traits. The 16 Types are commonly referred to by the initial letter of each of the four type preferences. The sole exception is Intuitive which is represented by the letter "N".

E Extrovert	I Introvert
High Energy	Quiet Energy
Talks More	Listens More
Outgoing	Ingoing
Enthusiastic	Reserved
Acts Before Thinking	Thinks Before Acting
Prefers Being With People	Comfortable Being Alone
Enjoys Public Roles	Enjoys Working Behind the Scene
S Sensor	**N Intuitive**
Detail Focused	Big Picture
Practical Solutions	Creative Ideas
Remembers Facts	Notices the New
What Is - Now	What Could Be - Future
Experience	Instincts
Established Skills - Instructions	New Ways - Figure It Out
Steady Pace	Bursts of Energy
F Feeler	**T Thinker**
Subjective - Emotional	Objective - Rational
Warm	Cool
Diplomatic	Direct
Harmony	Honesty
Compliment – Seeing Positives	Critical – Seeing Flaws
Appreciation	Accomplishment
Avoids Arguments	Attracts Arguments
P Perceiver	**J Judge**
Flexible	Planned
Spontaneous - Wing It	Scheduled - Prepared
Playful	Serious
Late	Prompt – On Time
Project Starter	Project Finisher
Play First	Work First
Indecisive	Decisive

Most of us are a little bit of each preference on the previous page, but we can find ourselves to be in one box or the other. Try identifying yourself and assigning a four letter sequence. I am an INTJ, meaning that I tend toward Introversion – Intuition – Thinking – Judging.

#1 ESFP	#5 - ESTP	#9 - ENFP	#13 - ENTP
Motivator-Presenter	Promoter-Executor	Discoverer-Advocate	Explorer-Inventor
Performer	Fun	Collaborative	Creative
Kinesthetic	Get-It-Done - Active	Visionary	Tenacious
Free-Spirited	Hands-On- Practical	Insightful	Funny - Clever
In The Moment	Observant	Spontaneous	Open
Fun	Outgoing - Talkative	Casual	Futuristic
Easy-Going	Take-Charge	Imaginative	Skeptical
Casual	Inventive	Sensitive	Independent
Entertaining	Charming	Energetic	Strategic
Sympathetic	Content	Gregarious	Unconventional
Warm - Emotional	Confident	Idealistic	Adaptable Easy Going
Outgoing – Talkative	Decisive	Disorganized	Disorganized
Spontaneous	Open	Spontaneous	Adventurous
Reckless	Crude	Irresponsible	Insensitive

#2 - ISFP	#6 - ISTP	#10 - INFP	#14 - INTP
Composer-Producer	Analyzer-Operator	Harmonizer-Clarifier	Designer-Theorizer
Free-Spirited	In The Moment	Sensitive	Independent
Unassuming	Quiet - Private	Caring - Healer	Analytical
Observant	Unflappable	Spontaneous	Private
Reserved	Calm Under Stress	Calm - Flexible	Unconventional
In The Moment	Down-to-Earth	Unique	Skeptical
Private	Concise	Reserved	Logic-Driven
Spontaneous	Realistic	Modest	Witty
Kind - Sensitive	Logic-Driven	Casual	Original
Quiet	Spontaneous	Empathetic	Internally-Motivated
Disorganized	Level-Headed	Creative	Disorganized
Modest	Unemotional	Idealist	Observer
Suggestible	Avoidant	Avoidant – Loner	Detached
Self-Pitying	Disorganized	Disorganized	Loner

#3 - ESFJ	#7 - ESTJ	#11 - ENFJ	#15 - ENTJ
Facilitator-Caretaker	Implementer-Leader	Envisioner-Mentor	Strategist-Mobilizer
Sensitive	Supervisor	Values-Driven	Tenacious
Talkative	Take Charge	Creative	Assertive
Responsible	Logical - Decisive	Affectionate	Strategic
Generous	Tenacious	Charismatic	Innovative
Attentive	Fast - Energetic	Planful	Proactive
Enthusiastic - Warm	Dependable	Social-Talkative	High Energy
Affectionate	Pro-Active	Idealistic	Bold
Sympathetic	Outspoken	Empathetic	Confident
Outgoing	Straight-Forward	Sensitive	Take Charge
Open	Organized	Emotional	Decisive
Easy to Read	Group Oriented	Altruistic	Dominant
Organized	Focused	Open	Ambitious
Shallow	Conventional	Manipulative	Stubborn

#4 - ISFJ	#8 - ISTJ	#12 - INFJ	#16 - INTJ
Protector-Supporter	Planner-Inspector	Foreseer-Developer	Conceptual-Strategist
Planful	Clear	Visionary	Mastermind
Decisive	Methodical	Creative	Independent
Reserved - Private	Loyal	Observer	Deep - Intellectual
Precise	Precise	Avoidant - Cautious	Intense - Driven
Sensitive-Sympathetic	Realistic	Sensitive - Empathetic	Future-Focused
Easily Offended	Reserved	Reserved	Tenacious
Literal	Meticulous	Private	Direct
Efficient	Responsible	Idealistic	Reserved - Private
Accommodating	Accurate	Planful	Perfectionist
Polite	Literal	Conscientious	Skeptical
Timid	Responsible	Values Driven	Observer
Obsessive	Private	Perfectionistic	Loner

"Every human being has a genius level talent. There are no chosen ones. You have to find what you're great at and tap into it."

~Jay-Z

CHAPTER 25
Probe

Your *STRENGTHSPATH SOLUTION* is in part discovered. You have a completely unique set of strengths. You were born with some of them and some have to be developed. Here is a list of the eight core strength types I usually start working on with a new client:

Passion (Deeply Embedded Life Interest, Deep Interest Structure, Enthusiasm, Desire, Ambition, Love, Fascinations, Magnificent Obsession, Energy, Excitement) Passions are activities and subjects that make you feel strong. Passions often include willingness to sacrifice and suffer.

Potential (Natural Ability, Aptitude, Gift, Knack, Flair, Bent, Instinct, Genius, Inclination, Brilliance, Forte, Aptness) Talent is a potential ability making performance and excellence at specific tasks easier. It also makes skill and knowledge acquisition easier with a specific domain.

Personality (Temperament, Preferences, Style, Nature, Disposition, Traits, Persona, Psyche) Personality is the organization of an individual's distinct traits and temperament.

Priorities (Values, Rewards, Motivation, Beliefs, Ideals, What's Important) Values are synonymous with priorities. They combine to build culture within an organization.

Processing (Learning Style, Perception, Organization, Retention and Response to Instruction Methods) You process information according to your unique learning style. It is your optimized pattern of acquiring and assimilating information.

Principles and Professional Terms (Knowledge, General Vocabulary, Industry Terminology, Rules, Regulations, Laws, Theories) Principles and professional terms are the acquired knowledge, information, facts, understanding and comprehension of a subject required in a particular kind of work.

Proficiencies (Skills, Developed Ability, Mastery, Competency, Know-How, How-To including Methods, Steps, Sequences, Tool Use, Technology Use) Proficiencies are skills. They are abilities developed through deliberate systematic effort, intentional practice and often supported by training and coaching.

Character (Honor, Morals, Ethics, Standards, Right/Wrong, Dependability, Attendance, Promptness) Character is keeping commitments, agreements and striving for excellence.

Most of us wander around completely oblivious to these *strengths and how they converge or integrate*. Yet, they can be clearly identified through a discovery process using a number of proven tools.

I've poured through hundreds of resources over the last 30 years looking at the different ways those active in career development help their employees, students or clients discover their strengths. There are several strengths discovery approaches that have a good track record. I recommend triangulating. Get three witnesses. Use many of the following methods for the most accurate results.

Autobiography Analysis

This is the basis of discovery. Writing about your life or telling an interested person your life story is a way identifying what you enjoy and what you excel at. Even a simple timeline representing each age of your life with a few notes can be useful. Jot down anything you can recall from each age. This will set the stage for the next analysis.

Achievement List Analysis

This method is very useful. I have often used a version of this in my workshops with what I call the *Factory Settings* exercise. I have class members list all the activities and subjects they either enjoyed or were good at, starting with their earliest memories. We then look for patterns of success, including activities, aptitudes and approaches that suggest any strengths. Bernard Haldane, Arthur Miller and Richard Bolles pioneered this approach. Each of these career counselors built programs around identifying personal success or achievement stories. They then helped their clients carefully review each story for patterns of passionate interest and ability. If you struggle with writing, substitute an interview process with a friend or family member.

Academic Analysis

Consider your grades and the coursework you most enjoyed. Include extra-curricular activities and independent reading preferences. Consider doing the **"Self-Designed Degree 120"** like *Whole Foods* founder John Mackey. He doesn't have a college degree, but he does have 120 units of college course work that interested him. Venture capitalist Randy Haykin shares that he took 16 classes at *Brown University* to find out which ones best resonated with his talents. Then he did the same thing at *Harvard*. Many think that college is best suited for developing your knowledge after you've figured out what you want to do. But it's actually a terrific place to experiment and discover your passion and in some cases your talents.

147

Assignment Analysis

Most jobs can be thought of as a single assignment or a series of assignments. Volunteering, paid or unpaid, for assignments that are outside your work history is a great way to experiment and expose yourself to potential strengths. You can do this for non-profit organizations or in corporate internships. My first published book started out as research and then a manual for a church class. I volunteered for two years as a community crisis counselor. My first trainer and coaching roles were unpaid. Try stuff!!! The secret of success is getting in alignment with your assignment - the one that fits. For most people this is a process of experimentation.

Activity List Analysis

This another effective strategy and works primarily with current tasks. Grab a sheet of paper and draw two lines creating room for three-column categories. The first category is for *Awesome Activities* that make you feel strong. The second category is for *Average Activities* that leave you feeling neutral. The third is *Awful Activities* that leave you drained. Every time you do an activity, place it in a category. Marcus Buckingham recommends a two-category version of this with his *Love It – Loathe It* exercise.

Anticipation Analysis

Peter Drucker used a method he borrowed from both the Jesuit and Calvinist faith communities. In the *Harvard Business Review* booklet, *Managing Oneself*, Drucker suggests, "Set a goal, anticipate the outcome and review the process for clues about your strengths." Drucker was arguably the top business consultant in the U.S., maybe the world, for several decades. He followed the process for 50 years, using it to identify the tasks he should take on and those he should leave for others.

Appraisal Analysis

Another method that can point you in the right direction is *Appraisal Analysis*. Any form of feedback including report cards, performance reviews, offhand compliments and requests to do work can all offer clues. Sometimes it can be helpful to ask those who know you best, "Hey, what do you see in me? What am I good at?" Motivational speaker Tony Robbins talks about a pivotal moment during his junior year of high school. One of his instructors, Mr. Cobb (no relation) came to him after speech class. Tony recalls that he looked into his eyes deeply, gave a long pause and said, "In all my years of teaching speech, I've never seen a student have more compelling power to move and influence people." Tony says, "Those words changed my life." Robbins continued, "Trying to use a strategy or be something you are not may deliver some results; it may work for a while, but being inauthentic long term, you aren't going to be happy. How do you take your talents and tie it into the role that is most aligned with those talents and maximize them, that ability is the real difference!"

Appearance Analysis

What keeps appearing in your life? What opportunities keep showing up at your front door? The ancient documents we sometimes refer to as the Old and New Testaments were written by over 40 authors over a 1500 year period. Many of these writings are what we might refer to as "Call and Response" narratives. At the end of the day, I believe in a Creator-God who has placed each of us on the planet with a specific purpose in mind. If you take those ancient documents seriously, as I do, you might consider the variety of ways He communicated those purposes including reoccurring dreams and orchestration of opportunities.

Assessments

My research suggests the Chinese were using vocational assessments 4,000 years ago. In the last 100 years, career counselors have used a variety of indicators to help with career discovery. I believe work sample assessments, like those offered by *Johnson O'Connor, Highlands Ability Battery* and Nicholas Lore's *Pathfinder Institute* are the most accurate for discovering aptitudes. But psychometric assessments, using trait choice, or more recently, situational judgment methods can be useful self awareness tools that will help you identify your unique work style approach. *Strengthsfinder 2.0, StandOut 2.0, Myers-Briggs* and *DISC* are all excellent choices. When debriefing a psychometric assessment report with a client, I always ask them to re-write any section they feel doesn't accurately describe them. **I use assessments because of the answers they suggest, but also because of the questions they raise.** Without assessments, those seeking to discover their STRENGTHSPATH must pull primarily from personal experience and an occasional burst of imagination.

Ability Analysis

Simply reading about aptitudes and their connection to careers can be very eye opening. I recommend reading through the abilities listed in *O*NET (Occupational Information Network)*. Go to https://www.onetonline.org/find/descriptor/browse/Abilities/ . You'll find descriptions of 21 Cognitive Abilities, 9 Physical Abilities, 10 Psychomotor Abilities and 12 Sensory Abilities. Many of the people and organizations that have built assessments also have books that describe aptitudes and approaches. Great books on aptitude include *Your Natural Gifts, Don't Waste Your Talent* and *The Pathfinder*. Great books on your approach talent include *Strengthsfinder 2.0, Stand Out 2.0, Type Talk at Work* and *People Smart.*

At the risk of being immodest, I believe my books *The STRENGTHSPATH Principle, The STRENGTHSPATH Time Manager, Dream Job,* and *Take This Job and Shape It* are excellent introductions to strengths discovery.

Answering Questions

Frank Parsons wrote *Choosing A Vocation* published in 1909, and oversaw the *Vocational Bureau* at the *Boston Y.M.C.A.*. He seems to have favored simply **Asking Questions** or using a structured set of inquiries. *Zen and The Art Of Making a Living* author Laurence Boldt says, "While traditional vocational guidance depends upon a testing process to identify your interests and/or skills, the new paradigm uses a series of carefully crafted questions designed to help you tap into your creative passion. You can take a test to discover a number of careers you may be suited for, but no test will ever tell you what you love to do - that you will have to discover for yourself. As a career coach I keep a list of great questions that assist me with strengths discovery process. One of my favorites is a variation of *The Miracle Question* created by Steve de Shazer and Insoo Kim Berg. It goes, "Suppose that after going to sleep tonight a miracle occurred. Imagine waking up tomorrow morning, and everything about your job had changed in the best way that you could imagine. Your work has shifted to something amazing overnight. What exactly would your job look like? What exactly would you see, hear, feel? **Most importantly, what would you be doing? How would you be doing it?** Where would you be doing it? Who would you be doing it with? How would you recognize that this is in fact your dream job?"

Animation Analysis

This is a great way to discover passion. What is the subject of discussion that causes you to wave your arms and pound your fists? What subjects get you all worked up? I sometimes refer to this as a "Lights On" moment. Tuning into your feelings about topics, tasks and types of problems can be an important clue. So can other physiological responses. What topics make your heart beat faster? What subjects raise your pulse rate? Entertainer and former *American Idol* judge Jennifer Lopez often talks about getting "goosies". *University of Maryland* President Freeman Hrabowski says, "When I do math problems I get goosebumps."

151

Susy and I have had the pleasure of visiting *Flags Up Farms*, just down the road from us in Solvang, California. The owner Monty Roberts, is a horse whisper who is known for his gentle training methods. In a conversation with *Chicken Soup for the Soul* author Jack Canfield, Roberts discussed his unique way of tuning into passion, "When I was in first, second, and third grade, I discovered that whenever I thought about doing something that really excited me, I got a very strong tingling sensation down in the depth of my stomach. This tingling in my belly also told me which direction to go at every crossroad in my life. I could just wait until the tingle came, and then I knew what the next step was."

Ask God

Shawn Askinosie was a very successful lawyer, one of only a handful who never lost a criminal case. But at one point he realized he couldn't do it anymore. He went to the doctor and then the hospital for chest pains. He ended up being diagnosed with chronic fatigue and saw a neurologist for three years. Shawn says that once he accepted that he had to leave law he began praying a very simple prayer, "Dear God, please give me something else to do." He says he prayed this prayer throughout the day for five years. Today Shawn is the founder and CEO of *Askinosie Chocolate*, an award-winning, craft, small batch, bean-to-bar chocolate factory located in Springfield, Missouri. He travels all over the world sourcing beans directly with farmers. Askinosie weaves social responsibility into every phase of the business. To read more of his story and get more insight on how he found his life's work, read *Meaningful Work: A Quest to Do Great Business, Find Your Calling, and Feed Your Soul.*

The strengths discovery process is not easy or short for most people. Economist Neil Howe believes that only 5% of people pick the right job on the first try. Some research suggests that in America, only 20% actually work in a career that is authentic for them. And most don't get in that role until they are 50 years of age or older.

In their book, *Discovering Your Career in Business,* Timothy Butler and James Waldroop write, "The type of work that will bring greater self knowledge, satisfaction and meaning is different for each of us, and each of us walks a different path of career discovery. As we grow through adulthood, two types of learning take place. The first type is learning about the world 'out there'; in business terms, this means learning about the different industries and work roles. The second type is learning about the self. Different psychologists have different definitions for self, but for our purposes we may say simply that the self is our developing consciousness of the full being that we are. As we grow older, we must do the work of making meaning, the work of discovering what is deeply satisfying and what activities consistently bring with them a sense of excitement, energy and connection with the world."

Butler and Waldroop continue, "It is a paradox that only by engaging in work can we discover what type of work is most satisfying and meaningful. Career self-assessment requires us to become better and better observers of ourselves as we learn about our individual psychological realities through day-to-day experience. With experience comes a greater ability to recognize more directly which tasks, assignments, and work opportunities are more likely to be fulfilling. Finding the best work is not a task that is accomplished once and for all; it is a continual process of doing, and listening to what we have learned and how we have changed because of our doing. We find our way to meaningful work by pursuing specific activities and, through them learning which are most fulfilling. Through activity our inner energies and enthusiasms find their way to the surface in our lives. Different aspects of the self are realized through different types of activities. For some people, writing a poem can be a powerful activity that increases self-knowledge. For others, mediating a worker argument on the production line or working on a new computer model of a national economy may be an equally powerful vehicle for self-realization."

I believe in the genius of all these methods and use each of them with my clients. Assessments in my view don't replace carefully crafted questions or achievement analysis. But neither do questions and achievement analysis fully replace assessments. They are bookends to a thorough and integrated discovery process. Questions and analyzing past achievements may do a better job mining the past for clues about one's strengths. Assessments on the other hand may unearth clues about potential topics and tasks that one hasn't experienced or even considered.

"Investing in yourself is the best thing you can do. Anything that improves your own talents; nobody can tax it or take it away from you. They can run up huge deficits and the dollar can become worth far less. You can have all kinds of things happen. But if you've got talent yourself, and you've maximized your talent, you've got a tremendous asset that can return ten-fold."

~Warren Buffet

CHAPTER 26
Polish

In order to fully realize potential, your natural success abilities must be polished, refined, grown, expanded, advanced, amplified and nurtured. Recent findings on the plasticity of the brain suggest that we can do this throughout life, even into old age.

Adaptive Modeling

List several role models here. Who are the experts already working at your Dream Job? Identify models of success. Discover the key fundamentals essential to their success. Develop a system that will allow you to incorporate the fundamentals into your life. Consistently apply those fundamentals to achieve success.

Steve Jobs said, "Expose yourself to the best things humans have done and then try to bring those things into what you are doing."

When Oprah Winfrey auditioned for her first television job, she was a nervous wreck. Oprah recalls, "I thought in my head that maybe I'll just pretend I'm Barbara Walters, I will sit like Barbara, I will hold my head like Barbara. So I crossed my legs at the ankles, and I put my little finger under my chin, and I leaned across the desk, and I pretended to be Barbara Walters."

The Beatles started as a cover band. Paul McCartney said, "I emulated Buddy Holly, Little Richard, Jerry Lee Lewis and Elvis. We all did.

We only started writing our own songs as a way to avoid other bands being able to play our set."

Henry Ford visited a meat processing plant and modified it for automobile manufacturing.

Sam Walton visited competitor stores and copied the best ideas. He was actually arrested while visiting South America because security found him on his hands and knees with a tape measure discovering the width of the aisles.

Amazon founder Jeff Bezos was obsessed with copying ideas from *Walmart*. He read from Sam Walton's book *Made In America* everyday.

Most people think that Edison invented the first light bulb. They're wrong. In fact, Edison was spectacularly late to the game. In 1878, when the 36-year-old inventor decided to focus on building a light bulb, 23 others had already invented early versions called arc lamps, some of which were being used commercially to light streets and large buildings.

Figure out ways to shadow or observe other people in your field. Learn from them. This includes their mistakes and weaknesses as well as their successes. Everyone is superior to me at something. I want to figure out what that something is, adopt it and then adapt it to fit my own strengths.

Active Reading - Become an Expert

Author Bob Philips once told me, "You can become an expert by reading 10 books on a subject." Put yourself on a reading/listening program depending on your learning style. Many books are available in recorded version. Develop a library of materials from the best people in your field. Find **Podcasts** and **Ted Talks** that relate to your interests and industry.

Excellence in business expert Tom Peters says, "Read deep! Read often! Out-READ the Competition!!!"

Warren Buffett's long-time partner Charlie Munger says, "In my whole life, I have known no wise people (over a broad subject matter area) who didn't read all the time—none, zero." Buffett himself says that he reads about six hours or 500 pages every day.

Bill Gates and Mark Zuckerberg are both huge readers who regularly share what they read and make recommendations.

Even as a teenager, *Tesla* founder Elon Musk reportedly read two books per day.

Jim Rohn said it well, "Poor people have big TVs. Rich people have big libraries."

When I say "Actively Read", I mean READ with a highlighter and take notes in the margins. Then transcribe or have transcribed the most useful sections of the material. I used index cards and an elaborate file system for decades but now I'm switching over to *Evernote*, an application I highly recommend.

Informational Interviews

Inspirational speaker Charlie "Tremendous" Jones used to say, "You'll be the same tomorrow except for the books you read and the people you meet." Talk with people already doing what you want to do. Conduct informational interviews with people already working in fields you are interested in. This can be done by phone or more ideally in person. Make sure that some of them are world class at what they do.

Classes

Sign up for a class at the university, community college, adult school or online options including *Khan Academy, Lynda, Coursera, Udemy* and *Udacity.* Find a workshop or seminar. Most classes are designed to increase knowledge more than skill but there are exceptions. *Dale Carnegie Courses* are skill oriented and touted by a lot of successful people including:

Johnny Cash – One of the most influential musicians of the 20th century

Emeril Lagasse – Celebrity chef, restaurateur and television personality

Warren Buffett – Considered the most successful investor of all-time

Mary Kay Ash – Founder of *Mary Kay Cosmetics*

Lee Iacocca – President and CEO of *Chrysler*

Scott Adams – Creator of the *Dilbert* comic strip

Rosalynn Carter – Former First Lady and advocate

Dr. Sanjay Gupta – *CNN's* medical expert

Chuck Norris – Actor, martial artist

Orville Redenbacher – Popcorn entrepreneur

Zig Ziglar – Motivational speaker

J.W. Marriott, Jr. – CEO of *Marriott Hotels*

Elliot Pete Estes – President of *General Motors*

Lyndon B. Johnson – 37th President of the United States

Bill Belichick – *New England Patriots* football coach

Tom Monaghan – *Domino's Pizza* founder

Tony Robbins – Motivational speaker

When I was 23, I cashed in a life insurance policy to pay for my *Dale Carnegie Course* tuition and consider it one of the best investments I ever made.

Join Your Tribe

Find your people. Go to **MeetUp.com** and see if there are meetings related to your field. If not, start one. Join groups dedicated to your field. Attend a convention. Join **LinkedIn** groups and start connecting with people who are already doing what you're doing or would like to be doing.

Deliberate Practice - Get Your 10,000 Hours

If you want to become the "Best-Version-Of-Yourself", you will need to practice! A popular modern concept is that you need 10,000 hours of deliberate practice to become a world-class performer in any field. This was first explored by *Florida State University* professor K. Anders Ericsson and then popularized by Malcolm Gladwell. Deliberate Practice is a highly structured activity designed to improve performance.

Skill - Deliberate practice focuses on a skill or skill set.

Strive – Deliberate practice constantly focuses on improvement.

Seek – Deliberate practice gets outside performance feedback.

Success – Deliberate practice evaluates results.

Role Play and Scrimmaging

I think of practice as more of a solitary event, while I think of role playing as something I usually do with a partner or a pretend audience. Martial Arts practice often involves role playing. A partner will take a pretend swing at you. Baseball, basketball and football teams have scrimmages that are designed to be a kind of "live" competitive form of practice.

At one time Ben Feldman was the top life insurance agent in the U.S., possibly the world. Ben would role play parts of his presentation with his wife at dinner every night.

Visualization and Mental Walk-Throughs

Whenever I give a talk or presentation, I generally do several mental walk-throughs. Usually this is in combination with practice and/or role playing. Maxwell Maltz wrote a book called *Psycho Cybernetics* that was published in 1960. It's sold tens of millions of copies since. One of the concepts Maltz talked about was something he called, *Theater of the Mind.* Maltz tells story after story of about successful people from all walks of life who utilize mental rehearsal. Maltz found he could actually improve performance by helping an individual "see" themself doing the activity perfectly in their mind.

One famous story about the power of visualization involves three teams of basketball players. One team practices making free throws. A second team doesn't practice. And a third team mentally visualizes making free throws. When the three teams are tested, the practice team out-scores the team that didn't practice. But, the team that mentally practiced with visualization performed nearly as well as the team that actually practiced.

Deliberate Experiments – Get Your 10,000 Failures

Thomas Edison famously had 10,000 light bulb failures before dialing it in. Deliberate practice works great building skills that are repeatable, especially like those in sports and music. Some work, by its very nature, is highly experimental. If your job requires frequent change like in sales, business and technology, you will need to fail fast and keep moving. Five years of practicing the same thing would insure a salesperson would be off the cutting edge. In my work as a sales representative I used a structured outline and practiced it. But unfortunately, my customers never seemed to practice their part of the script. As a result, I needed to continually experiment and try out new ideas. Try stuff and record your results!

Get "Feed-Forward" Not "Feed-Back"

Feed-Back can be useful and most of us can benefit from reflecting on both past wins and losses. But at the end of the day, the most hopeful input you can receive is about the one thing you can impact...the future. World class business coach Marshall Goldsmith makes a big deal of this "Feed-Back" "Feed-Forward" distinction and it's central to his coaching practice. He has worked with over 10,000 leaders on this one idea alone. His strategy is simple:

1. **Pick** a behavior you'd like to change.

2. **Ask** for "Feed-Forward". Solicit suggestions for the future that might help achieve positive change with the selected behavior.

3. **Listen** attentively to the suggestions and take notes.

4. **Thank** the person warmly for the suggestion while <u>NOT</u> commenting either positively or negatively on the perceived validity of the ideas proposed. Simply thank them for their input.

Goldsmith believes two minutes is the optimal time frame for the exchange. He claims that participants listen more attentively to Feed-Forward, are much less defensive when receiving it and the strategy avoids negative stereo-typing and negative self-fulfilling prophecies.

Give it a try!

"Packaging can be theater, it can create a story."

~Steve Jobs

Chapter 27
Package

Think of yourself and your set of strengths as a product. As important as the product itself is, it can be just as important to package yourself and your strengths well. *Apple* invests incredible amounts of money to provide the best computers and smart phones available. But they also invest a lot of money to make sure that those products are packaged and displayed with excellence. This starts with the wrapping and boxes and images but also includes the stores and displays.

Starbucks invests incredible amounts of money to source and serve a great cup of coffee. But they also invest money to make sure that coffee is served in attractive paper products and in compelling café environments.

Joshua Bell is a world class violinist. Playing in his normal concert hall venues, he makes thousands of dollars for each performance. As an experiment, he played in street clothes and a baseball hat at a subway station for a few hours, receiving compensation from commuters. For his efforts in the subway venue he made a little over thirty dollars. What was the difference? Packaging!

How are you packaging yourself and your strengths? A portfolio is a grouping of evidence that showcases your preparation—examples and copies—of anything you've worked on and/or accomplished in school, at a job, or in volunteer work. For many candidates, a portfolio offers a comfortable way of demonstrating ability with "real life" examples.

Sales trainer Brian Tracy emphatically says, "Use visual sales aids, thy are 15 times more powerful than words. The average attention span of the average prospect is 3 sentences." I completely agree. While visuals can be overdone… most of us have experienced "death by PowerPoint", in general, relevant images hold our attention.

Portfolios have been used by many professionals to describe, display and demonstrate their developed knowledge and skill. Possible inclusions depending on your specific career target might include:

- Evidence of relevant accomplishments
- Achievement List
- Certificates
- Product Certifications
- Transcripts
- Technical Journals
- Performance evaluations/annual reviews from past jobs
- Evidence of client satisfaction
- Reference letters
- Work samples **– Including *YouTube* Videos**
- Detailed challenge descriptions with solutions
- Evidence of certain skills
- List of technical skills such as software programs
- Goals and 5-year plan
- Descriptions of projects
- Pictures of projects
- Other relevant photos
- Charts and graphs demonstrating success
- Honors/Awards
- Innovations
- Sample training programs
- Lifelong learning list
- Relevant reading list

Resume Packages

To review, a complete resume package will include several pieces if you want to **stand out** from other candidates and increase your chances of getting hired. The pieces may include:

- Master resume
- Targeted resume customized to a specific position
- Master cover letter
- Targeted cover letter customized to a specific position
- Reference sheet with contact information
- Endorsement sheet with brief comments on your work
- Reference letters from co-workers, customers and employers
- Interview leave behind packet
- Portfolio which may include all of the above plus target position description, certificates, school transcripts and work samples

Every resume and every resume package should be a unique one-of-a-kind set of documents!!!

A resume package is an ongoing living description of who you are, your special strengths, what you can contribute and how you add value!

Keep your resume package updated and customize it for the specific role and specific company you are applying into.

The generic one-size-fits-all resume is dead! Please re-read that statement until it sinks into your subconscious.

This change occurred slowly. Years ago a resume was assembled with a description of work history and was delivered by mail or often brought with you to the initial interview. Most people would use the same resume regardless of what position they were applying for. Progressively, the computer has driven the change. Today, word processors like *Microsoft Word* allow almost anyone to customize their resume for a specific job opening relatively quickly. Over time it has become the norm. In other words, customization is expected.

Robert Half International suggests, "Rather than creating a standard document that you submit to every company that interests you, tailor your resume to each opportunity. Use the job description as your guide, emphasizing your background and abilities that closely match what the company is looking for. This may mean placing more focus on your 'certifications' and 'strong presentation skills' for one perspective employer, while playing up your 'self-directed' nature and 'proven ability to be effective with minimal supervision' for another."

Every time you deliver a resume, either electronically, by mail or in person, it should be customized.

"Nothing happens until somebody sells something."

~Thomas J. Watson

Chapter 28
Promote

It's ironic that I have over two decades of experience in sales and sales management but I still find I'm writing this chapter from a place of weakness. I'm writing it for those interested in business startup and entrepreneurship but most of the principles can be applied to any job search. For more strategies on job search I recommend my book, *Dream Job – A Strengths Based Guide to Finding Work You Love.*

In my early 20s, I worked one year for the *Zig Ziglar Corporation.* For almost a decade, I worked as a self-employed contractor. The way I got most of my business was cold-calling interior designers and paint stores who gave me referral business. I then worked for a well-known national company as an outside sales representative where I made thousands of cold calls for another decade. Eventually I advanced into work as a sales trainer and sales manager and was reasonably successful in each of those roles.

But I never became either confident or comfortable with the initial sales call, walking into the office of a complete stranger and asking for the opportunity to present my product and service. As I've moved into the world of writing books and coaching, I've found it even harder, as I became the product.

So if you're stuck on this one, I get it. Still, I've got a lifetime of experience to share and I believe some wisdom that will help.

So let's get started…

First, much of what passes as sales training is not helpful. And a lot of salespeople are very poor representations or role models of effective selling. So don't go to the car lot looking for a good role model. There are a few great salespeople selling cars, but in my experience they are few and far between. This is true for a lot of other products and services as well. Good salespeople are very rare.

Most of the books on selling are not helpful either. But there are a few very good ones. Here are a few of my favorites:

The Tao of Sales by E. Thomas Behr
Purple Cow by Seth Godin
Go-Givers Sell More by Bob Burg and John David Mann
Selling with Noble Purpose by Lisa Earle McLeod
Changing The Game by Larry Wilson
The One Minute Sales Person by Larry Wilson
Stop Selling - Start Partnering by Larry Wilson
Win-Win Selling by Larry Wilson
It's Not What You Sell It's What You Stand For by Roy M. Spencer
The Versatile Salesperson by Roger Whenschlag
Conceptual Selling by Robert B. Miller and Stephen E. Heiman
Strategic Selling by Robert B. Miller and Stephen E. Heiman
The Trusted Advisor by David H. Maister and Charles H. Green
Selling the Invisible by Harry Beckwith

These books are generally in the "Servant Selling" category. They generally recommend non-manipulative strategies that are not trying be gamey or coy.

If you are going to be your own salesperson, you may need to make a lot of sales calls. There is no substitute for being aggressive. But by aggressive I mean making a lot of calls. Don't ever be rude or pushy. Go out with the mindset of "exposing" your product or service, never "imposing". There is no such thing as hard sell or soft sell. There is only smart sell and stupid sell. Treat every potential customer like they are your favorite relative. Be polite and respectful. In spite of what a lot of sales trainers tell you, you *will* need to learn to take no for an answer… probably a lot. Don't burn bridges. Try to leave it where whoever you speak with will be happy to see you again. A lot of sales are made on the 10th or 15th call. I made sales on accounts that took me 5, 6, 7 years. In one case, after I became a manager and hired my replacement, I helped him make a sale on an account that I had worked on for 8 years.

In football terminology, think about the long drive where you pick up 4, 5 or 6 yards on every sales call you make. You may throw a long pass for a touch down occasionally, but it's not how most football teams score touchdowns and it's not how most sales are made.

As a salesperson and then as a sales manager, I realized there were essentially three things that would increase sales:

See More People
See Better People
See People Better

Let's take them one at a time.

See More People – As I said on the previous page, you may need to make a lot of sales calls when you start out. In my industry, I made 20 to 30 face-to-face calls a day at the beginning. I occasionally ran "Full-Throttle" campaigns where I increased my call level. If you're selling by phone, you may need to make over 100 dials a day. A lot of calls in one sales industry may vary if you're working in another.

See Better People – Seeing better people just means spending more time calling on accounts who are more likely to buy. This can be tricky to understand when you are starting out. But over time you'll want to work on figuring out the type of people or accounts who are most likely to buy and spend the majority of your time with them. In the sales world, this is often called "qualifying" or spending time with "qualified prospects". It may be based on the size of a business or the economic level of the potential client. Spending a lot of time with people who can't afford your product or service is not moving you toward a sale. On the other hand, politely investing a small amount of time in someone who may grow into a qualified buyer is smart.

It's not always obvious who is qualified. In the 1990s I went to lunch with one of *Saturn's* top salespeople. Kay told me a story about a lady who walked onto the showroom floor. She wasn't dressed particularly well and the other salespeople scattered. Kay introduced herself and politely showed the woman the different car models. At the end of her presentation, the woman opened her purse and paid for the vehicle with cash. It always pays to be polite.

Seeing People Better – This is anything and everything you do when you show up. It's improving how appropriately you dress for the specific clientele you serve. If you're opening a surf shop, appropriate is something different than opening a high-end clothing store. It may even mean improving how appropriate your car is for the audience you're trying to relate to. Almost no detail is too insignificant to overlook.

Seeing People Better is primarily about your presentation or presentations. It's continually looking for ways to improve how you present yourself and your product or service. You'll probably want to develop a very brief 20 second presentation to use with the receptionist or whoever meets you when you walk in the door. I recommend having a few different versions of your full presentation that you'll use with a decision maker. Some potential clients want a lot of detail and others don't. You'll want to learn to read people and customize the length to their individual preferences. When your prospect starts to fidget or asks you to get to the point, you've taken too long.

You'll want to make your presentation as interactive as possible. Learn to ask a few good questions, listen carefully and then ask a few follow up questions. If you can involve the potential client in the presentation that can

174

be very helpful. Whatever you do, make sure you're not the one doing all the talking.

I hate the word "Pitch". It makes you think about selling as something you do to your future client. You want to do it with them. You may lead the conversation, but you should also encourage them to lead and create an environment where they will ask you questions.

I don't recommend that you memorize a sales presentation verbatim. I did this when I went to work for the *Zig Ziglar Corporation* in 1979. It was 20 pages single spaced and one of the hardest things I've ever done. But I don't think it was effective either.

I do recommend building a repeatable outline of no more than 8 points. Build a repeatable sequence and find some phrases that clearly communicate the unique features, benefits and value you offer. This will probably take some time and a lot of experimenting with real clients.

Conceptual Selling by Robert B. Miller and Stephen E. Heiman is a terrific resource for building your presentation. Miller and Heiman simplify the sales process into 3 parts – Getting Information, Giving Information and Getting Commitment.

Forget about "Overcoming Objections". Like "Pitch", it makes you think about doing something to your future client, or manipulating them, instead of working with them. Miller and Heiman talk about "Resolving Concerns". This is a much more effective way to think about selling. Clients will have concerns and you will need to resolve them. When you start trying to overcome objections, you will often end up in an argument. And arguments rarely end up in a sale.

From a strengths perspective, there will probably be parts of the sales process you're good at and parts you're not good at. There will be parts you enjoy and parts you don't enjoy. Consider trying to outsource the parts you don't enjoy. If you like making presentations but don't enjoy contacting strangers to set appointments, hire an appointment setter and split the profits. If you're good with a computer, try getting leads with online marketing. Advertise instead of cold calling.

"The important element here is DELIVER. Many people have good ideas, good intentions, even produce good products or services, but either their value is not considered very valuable in today's marketplace, or they just don't deliver enough of it."

~T. Harv Eker

Chapter 29
Perform

Action, performance and contribution is the endgame of *The STRENGTHSPATH Solution*. A lot of people take strengths assessments, throw them in a drawer and never see them again. Seth Godin describes a similar phenomena with what he calls "Transformational Tourism":

"I bought the diet book, but ate my usual foods."
"I filled the prescription, but didn't take the meds."
"I took the course... well, I watched the videos... "
"Merely looking at something almost never causes change. Tourism is fun, but rarely transformative."

And Timothy Butler warns, "Recognizing the deeper patterns of the self is not enough. We must find the will to act, even in very small ways, so that our new imagination becomes more and more what we live everyday."

Delivering your strengths, by executing your unique approaches, using your aptitudes and implementing activities that make you feel strong, are the critical steps to realizing your full potential.

But it's critical to remember, performance is ALWAYS the point. The purpose of your strengths is to make a contribution to add value to others.

Marketplace Contributions include things like:

Helping the employer or client **make money**

Helping the employer or client **save money**

Helping the employer or client **reach an important goal**

Helping the employer or client **avoid or solve a problem**

Support someone who does one of the above

Ways to Add Value

As I mentioned in the last chapter, when I was a sales manager and regional trainer for a large national company, I consistently worked with salespeople around three concepts or ideas:

See more people - Efficiency

See better people - Effectiveness

See people better - Excellence

One, how could the salespeople see more people, more prospects, more potential clients or customers? Two, how could they see better people – meaning more qualified or likely to buy? Three, how could they see people better – give more compelling presentations?

E-Tickets

Susy and I are *Disney* fans. On my 60th birthday she took me to the *Walt Disney Museum* in San Francisco. Truly, it was a thrilling day! One of our purchases in the gift shop was a large replica of the old *E-Ticket*. The phrase *E-Ticket* (or *E -Ticket* ride) refers to the ticketing system used at *Disneyland* from 1959 to 1982 when it admitted the bearer to the newest, most advanced, and/or most popular rides and attractions. Original *"E-Ticket"* rides included the *Monorail*, the *Matterhorn Bobsleds* and the *Submarine Voyage*. Eventually, this special ticket included other rides like *It's A Small World*, *Pirates of the Caribbean* and *Jungle Cruise*.

With that in mind, think of the following ways to advance your career or business. How could you create your own version of the *E-Ticket*?

Efficiency

The first question is an efficiency question. In sales, efficiency is often about seeing more people. But efficiency is important in every role.

Efficiency is about staying organized, working faster, getting more done in a shorter amount of time. Efficiency means accomplishing more tasks or completing more projects.

It doesn't mean rush. In fact, in some cases, efficiency might mean you need to slow down. Basketball coach John Wooden always said, "Be quick but don't hurry." Fred Smith, who was the founder of *Fed Ex*, arguably knows quite a bit about efficiency. Smith says, "Too often people don't know the difference between the fast track and the frantic track."

In my work as a salesperson, then as a sales manager and later as a career coach, I instigated "Full-Throttle" campaigns. Usually these were single week "Sprints" focused on speed and efficiency. In sales that meant making 100 or more customer contacts or 20 outside sales calls per day. In our context, this was double the typical daily regimen. In job search, a "Full-Throttle" campaign might mean a "Sprint" or single week focused on one aspect of job search.

Effectiveness

The second question is the effectiveness question. Effectiveness is about working on the right tasks or projects. It's about getting the right things done. It's about spending time with the right people. While efficiency is about completing more, effectiveness is about working on tasks with the most pay-off. Peter Drucker spent most of his consulting career hammering away on the theme of effectiveness. Drucker wrote, "There is nothing so useless as doing efficiently that which should not be done at all."

Excellence

The third question is the excellence question. Excellence is all about increasing the quality. It's about getting things done right. I always think about any presentation or project in terms of:

Basic – Generic
Better – Improved
Best – Top of the Line
Break-Through – Never Been Done Before

It's okay to start out with Basic. We all start there and build. Japan started out building cars that were basic transportation. Over time, *Honda* and *Toyota* got better. After a little more time they became the Best. In

179

terms of quality and defects, they were both Break-Through. How did they do that? There are a lot of answers to that question. In *Toyota's* case, they are a strengths based organization. They have focused on employee strengths for years. They also implemented over one million employee improvement ideas in a single year.

In a sales context, working with representatives on building or refining a quality sales presentation was one of the things I did best. I helped reps use visuals and wording that was both high quality and hyper-targeted to different prospects and customers. In some ways I was obsessed with this.

Efficiency, Effectiveness and Excellence were my original three. Since then, I've added a few new performance enhancing attractions.

Elegance

I think of elegance as a visual extension of excellence. When I hear the word elegance, I think of design. Elegance is about beauty and style. Increasingly, elegance is about simplicity. Steve Jobs said, "When you first start off trying to solve a problem, the first solutions you come up with are very complex, and most people stop there. But if you keep going, and live with the problem and peel more layers of the onion off, you can often times arrive at some very elegant and simple solutions."

Experience

Like elegance, customer experience may be an extension of excellence. Increasingly it is a dimension that is a neglected aspect of doing business or improving business. Everyone has a customer, sometimes it's an internal customer within the company and sometimes it's an external customer like a client. If you are a teacher, your students are your customers. If you work at a church, the attendees are your customers.

I like to think of experience in terms of what some call "The Customer Journey". The customer journey is a series of "Touchpoints" or "Moments of Truth". The first moment of truth or touchpoint is always the "GoesInto", that place where the customer or prospective customer Goes-Into the experience. It's the first impression of you, your product or your service. It could be your phone call, your initial visit, your signage, your website, your advertisement or your book cover.

One way to think more clearly about all this is to create a simple customer journey map. Fold an 8.5x11 sheet of paper in half three times.

180

Then unfold the paper leaving you with eight sections. Create headings at the top of each section representing different customer touchpoints or moments of truth. Think about each touch, moment or customer interaction. How could it be better?

Performance is always the point of your strengths. And performance is all about increasing the value you add and the contributions you make.

"When you find something you're truly passionate about, it will prioritize itself."

~Karen X. Cheng

Chapter 30
Persevere

What is the role of persistence and discipline in strengths based career development? This is really a crux-of-the-matter question. A high percentage of us find ourselves in jobs where the tasks we're good at and enjoy, are not what we're hired to do.

As Steve Jobs reminded us, success is really hard. Working in our passions while applying our talents, doesn't remove hard work. I love to write and I've been at it here for the last five hours with almost no breaks. My legs are about to cramp and my brain is getting close to being fried. But I love it. I have a certain talent for doing research and arranging thoughts on paper. I'm working on improving the skill dimension. My wife helps with grammar, spelling and an occasional content adjustment for better communication. It's hard work. But it's hard work I love. There is a certain persistence and discipline about it, or as Vishen Lakhiani calls it, *Blissipline*.

Next, there is the persistent discipline of staying in your strengths. The insistence on working in your strengths is still very much a counter-cultural revolutionary act in some circles. The lazy misinformed mantra in both the classroom and the boardroom is that, "Anyone can do anything. If you're not successful, you're just not working at it." Part of my mission is to change that.

Also, there is the persistent discipline of doing tasks that are clearly out of your strengths zone. The transition to a strengths based life is a work in progress. Bill Hendricks has been working for a couple of decades helping others make strengths based career transitions. He's worked with thousands of clients and estimates it takes five to seven years to make a complete transition. There will be disappointments, defeats and setbacks just like any other area of life.

Procrastination

Jessica Hische is an American letterer, illustrator, and type designer. She wisely writes, **"The work you do while you procrastinate is probably the work you should be doing for the rest of your life."** This is the best insight I've ever heard on procrastination. When you're not working on what you're "supposed to be working on", what is it you do?

What is the work you do when you're procrastinating? That's probably something close to what God put you on the planet to work on. What do you keep gravitating towards? What keeps pulling you back? This is a great place to look for career guidance. Some version of this topic or task has probably been pulling at you since you were a child.

In my case, I was pretty good at writing papers in school. I still remember my first speech in 6th grade and it was a very positive experience. When I was working as a contractor, I kept my shirt pocket full of 3x5 cards. I'd scribble down notes for writing as I worked on construction projects. I couldn't help it. I had to get the ideas out of my head and onto paper. I still have some of those cards 30 years later and that information is part of this book.

So my first advice on procrastination is to look at it as a huge potential message from God about what you're really supposed to be doing with your life. But don't quit your day job. As I said in the last chapter, there may be a multi-year transitional process ahead.

Career coach Christine Mims talks about what she calls, "Passion Clumps". She writes, "Passion clumps is the idea that finding your passion and building a fulfilling career is rarely a short and linear experience. Instead, you do some stuff, think about some stuff, get angry or frustrated about other stuff, do more stuff again, and the insight comes *in bursts over time, with effort.* In other words, progress to your passion happens most often in clumps." This is such a brilliantly accurate description of career transitions. They are often messy. Her role, as well as mine, is to speed up the clumpiness and get you into the career that fits faster.

There will be times that you're procrastinating and you just need to get it done. Time management expert Alan Lakein recommends when you are having trouble putting off a high priority task, commit to doing nothing until and unless you begin that task. Give it a try.

On his uber popular website *43folders*, Merlin Mann suggests a *SUCCESSPATH* Math technique he calls (10+2)*5. It's 10 minute work boxes, 2 minute break boxes, repeated 5 times. Try it.

I don't believe you will ever maximize your success until you are spending most of your work hours on something that excites you. You can only operate from pure discipline for so long, and then it's exhausting. When you love what you do, you will jump out of bed every morning and will be excited to get to work. And as a result, you will succeed more often. Passion will automatically drive you to work smarter, harder and longer. You will endure failures with comeback after comeback. And that's great career management.

"Parts are a portion of the unconscious mind, which often have conflicting beliefs and values."

~Tad James

Chapter 31
Parts

In her book, *Mindworks*, trainer Anne Linden explains what *Neuro-Linguistic Programing (NLP)* practitioners call "Parts". Linden says, "By 'parts' I mean aspects or qualities of a person: the efficient part, the stay-at-home part, the nurturing part, the shopper part, the baby, the glamour girl and all the other selves, parts and facets that make up the whole individual, whether or not the person is conscious of them."

Learning to integrate these parts is the artistic side of career development. Like the snowflake, you are a completely unique, one-of-a-kind individual. This is why off-the-rack jobs always need some tailoring, just like a well-made suit of clothes.

Learning to integrate your parts, especially those in tension will require wisdom and some trial and error. It's a little like the story of the wizard and the magic carpet:

A younger wizard wanted a magic carpet just like the old wizard. The old wizard agreed to help and show the young wizard how to weave his own. When the magic carpet was complete, the young wizard was disappointed because it was very plain. The old wizard explained, "The more experiences you have, the wiser you become, the richer and more beautiful your carpet becomes."

Integrating all our parts, including the passions, talents, skills, knowledge and values with their inevitable tensions is like that.

Think about your current roles. What are the tasks you perform on an hourly, daily, weekly or monthly basis? Would you hire you?

Bridgewater Investments founder Ray Dalio talks about the You #1 and You #2 Concept. The writing is a little confusing at first but stay with it. I think you'll find it highly valuable. Imagine there are two of you...

You #1 – A Coach = You as the designer and overseer of the plan to achieve your goals.

You #2 – A Player = You as one of the participants in pursuing those goals.

You #1 sees You #2 as one of many resources to get what You#1 wants done.

To be successful, You #1 has to be objective about You #2.

Let's imagine that your goal is to have a winning basketball team. Wouldn't it be silly to put yourself in a position that you don't play well? If you did, you wouldn't get what you want. Whatever your goals are, achieving them works the same way.

If You #1 sees that You #2 is not capable of doing something, it is only sensible for You #1 to have someone else do it. In other words, You #1 should look down at You #2 and all the other resources at You #1's disposal and create a "machine" to achieve You #1's goals.

Remember that You #1 doesn't necessarily need to do anything other than design and manage the machine to get what You #1 wants. If You #1 finds that You #2 can't do something well, fire You #2 and get a good replacement!

You #1 shouldn't be upset that You #2 is bad at that. You #2 should be happy because You #1 has improved You #1's chances of getting what You #1 wants. If You #1 is disappointed because You #2 can't be the best person to do everything, You #1 is terribly naive because nobody can do everything well.

The biggest mistake most people make is to not see themselves and others objectively. If they could just get around this, they could live up to their potential.

In the early days of professional sports, player coaches were actually fairly common. The most recent example was Bill Russell, who for a time both played and coached the *Boston Celtics* basketball team.

Business coach Marshall Goldsmith talks about a similar concept he calls the "Planner-Doer". Goldsmith shares, "We display **two discreet personas I call 'planner' and 'doer'.** The planner who wakes up in the morning with clear plans for the day is not the same person later in the day who has to execute those plans…. Basic tools such as anticipating, avoiding, and adjusting to risky environments are a good place to start correcting this conflict between planner and doer in us."

"Success comes to those who run their own race, at their own pace, on their own track."

~ Tom Volkar

CHAPTER 32
Pace

Tortoises and hares can both be winners… but only if they learn to be their best selves. I tend to be a steady plodding tortoise. I can muster up a hare's speed for up to a week and maybe two weeks at a time. Beyond that, it doesn't work for me. A guaranteed path to failure is to impose a time temperament on yourself that doesn't fit who you are. Another path to failure, is to impose your time temperament on someone else.

I'm purely talking about your overall day-in day-out flow of activity. If you are a sprinter then sprint. If you are a marathoner then work in harmony with who God made you. There are gold medalists in both types of events. This concept is contrasted with giving 100% - 100% of the time. The world's fastest man can't maintain sub 10-second 100-meter dash speeds while running a 440. Usain Bolt is currently the world's fastest man… in the 100-meter dash. He has never even run a full mile. He focuses on the races he can win.

All high achievers pace themselves. When Tiger Woods was playing the best golf of his career, he didn't play every tournament. In the course of a year, he took several weeks off. He focused on four major tournaments that included the *Masters*, the *U.S. Open*, the *British Open* and the *PGA Championship*.

Dr. Bob Rotella is one of America's top sports psychologists and has worked with many elite athletes, rock stars and business leaders. Bob says, "If you think trying your hardest is what doing your best is all about, you're confused. You must make a decision to throw away any attitudes that sound good and look good but don't work."

Former *Navy Seal* instructor, Richard "Mack" Machowicz agrees. In his book *Unleash The Warrior Within* he writes, "You often hear the expression 'giving it your all' or 'giving 110 percent effort.' I don't believe in thinking that way, or training that way. You can't put 110 percent into anything because it's against the laws of physics. You only have 100 percent, and I believe that the closer you push yourself to 100 percent, the closer you are to shutting your body down. You can run your car at top speed for a few seconds, but after that it starts to shake, and ultimately falls apart. The more effective way to think is to aim for bringing all your skills to 80 percent of your maximum, in whatever you do. At this point you are able to think, to use your body to stay in balance and harmony, to flow rather than force. In sports performance, researchers call this the 'steady state,' because your body systems are running at an efficient level."

I agree with "Mack" on this completely and I would only add that 80% looks different for different people. Sometimes I take an electronic metronome into my Time Management Classes. I turn the speed up and down between:

Tic...Tic...Tic and **Tic............Tic..............Tic.**

Not only is everyone different in what they can productively maintain, they are unique in each season of life.

Time Shifting - Task Synchronization

Many tasks have an optimal rhythm built into them. When I hung wallpaper, I had to set my pace to the unique qualities of the material. Vinyl worked quickly. Paper was a little slower. Foils were extremely slow.

Sometimes that rhythm is a combination of your time temperament and how it fits together with the task itself. In the case of a sales call or classroom presentation, it may be syncing up your temperament with the temperament of others. You may also need to sync up with the type of information.

Every presentation has an optimal pace, time frame (duration), time of day, and arrangement of content that is unique or different from any other. Discovering these factors and aligning with them may get you a lot of business.

Other more mundane tasks like putting together information packets also have an optimal rhythm. You could get faster, but faster isn't always better.

"Maximizing efficiency and getting the most out of your work day may depend on recognizing the best times for you to perform certain tasks."
~Kathy Rembisz

Chapter 33
Prime-Time

Every position or role has a prime time. This is defined as a window that is disproportionately effective in performing a core payoff activity. In my outside selling, the core payoff activity was calling on prospective customers for the purpose of securing new business. In my industry, prime time was 9 am until 1 pm. More business could be gathered in this time window than any other. Every industry is a little different on the specific time window. But let me assure you, your industry has a prime time.

If you sell into different industries then you may have multiple prime times, one for each industry. If you don't know what this is in the industry you work in, then find out quickly. When you figure it out, work hard to focus all your core activity into prime time.

Chronotype - Your Personal Prime Time

Personal prime time is the window when you are individually most awake, alert, and physically strong. My personal prime time matched up very closely with the industry prime time that I sold into. **To maximize effectiveness, so should yours. This time window is based on your own biological or circadian rhythms.** Are you a morning person or a night person? Are you a lark or an owl? Some people think they can go both ways. Maybe they can, but they might be fooling themselves. **You may be able to adjust it slightly by adjusting your bedtime** but on the whole, you are probably stuck with your unique personal prime time.

If you don't match up well, you should at least consider shifting into a career that better fits. If you are a hiring manager, ask questions about personal prime time when interviewing a new candidate. You want them to have every natural advantage possible when they first start out and hopefully continue for a long career.

I recommend a deeper dive on this topic. Read the book, *The Power of When*, by board certified sleep doctor Michael Breus. Start with his free chronotype assessment which you can find on the internet at thepowerofwhen.com . You will discover if your sleep patterns more closely resemble the lion, the bear, the dolphin or the wolf. Have each family member and everyone on your team take the quiz and then make appropriate adjustments to align with their natural chronotype. According to Dr. Mehmet Oz, who wrote the introduction, those adjustments could even save their life.

Your Main Event

Every day should have a main event or task, one that is more important than all the rest. Every week should have a main event or task as well. These high priority events, by some criteria, are more important to your success than the others in any given day or week.

For the most part, your main events should align heavily with your main strengths. They will be based on your highest passion and biggest talent. Your main event should consistently line up with your personal prime time.

If you are calling on an account that can produce $100,000 in sales and an account that can produce $10,000 in sales, you need to invest more preparation in the larger account. I once spent nearly a whole week preparing for a presentation to the largest account in my territory. The extra preparation paid off. We landed the account.

This is not an excuse to slack on service or preparation with the $10,000 account. It simply means extra preparation for the larger one.

Your main events should showcase your core strengths. Again, if there is a close match between your strengths and task/events, that will insure your success.

"Much of your day is spent in between activities... Between meetings... Before appointments… Waiting in line... And more. Making use of this time can make all the difference."

~Craig Jarrow

CHAPTER 34
Plant

My Grandpa Burns was a brilliant man with several patents to his name even though he only had a grammar school education. He got his start as a farm laborer. He went to his employer one day and asked if he could plant cotton between rows of the young walnut trees he was tending. He got the approval and that was his start as a farmer.

What can you plant in between rows? Where are the spaces in your life? Which spaces if properly utilized could be turned into profit for you and your family? Much of this book was written in the spaces of my life. Much of it was written one 3x5 card at a time in odd moments. This isn't unusual with authors. John Bunyan wrote *Pilgrim's Progress* on milk jug covers that his wife brought to him while he was in prison. J.K. Rowling had the inspiration to write *Harry Potter* while waiting for a four hour train delay. Much of the early writing took place in what Rowling called "stolen moments at a café table". I may not have J.K. Rowling's ability to craft a sentence, but I have utilized her strategies and so can you. Most of my books were written, in large part, during my time gaps.

An average game in professional sports lasts approximately three hours on television. If you know something about football, basketball and baseball, these games are full of timeouts with moments in-between quarters, halves and innings. In other words, actual play time is about 1/3 of total time.

That gives you two hours of time that you could spend on something profitable during a game. You could probably read several inspirational books during football season and never miss a play. You could outline or write a chapter for that book you've been meaning to write. You could write thank you notes to associates, volunteers, customers, employees, and anyone else who contributes to your life. You might memorize passages from the Bible.

You may be saying, "Dale, you're missing the point...football is my down time... I just want to relax and enjoy the game." Well then, you're missing my point. I'm just using football as an example. Everyone has spaces that can be packed with something profitable. And a nap is profitable. So is relaxation. I'm just asking you to consider all the spaces in your life and invest in some of them.

Make sure all or most of this space time is either invested in using your strengths or freeing up time that can be used on your strengths at another point.

The Waiting Kit

For many years I've kept a waiting kit with me. In some seasons it was a formalized pack of reading and writing material. I always have several books in my car. Usually my reading material is connected to what I'm currently writing about so that there is an interplay between reading and writing.

I have my waiting kit with me for every doctor's appointment. It has grown more digital over the years. I store books on my *iPad* and career oriented apps on my phone. I check email while standing in line. I keep a list of my signature strengths, my signature goals and writing outlines in *Trello*. I also review articles and other items in *Evernote*.

Windshield Time

How long is your commute? Maybe for you, it's in a carpool or your windshield is at the front of the subway train or airplane. For eight years of my life, I was in and out of airplanes and airports. Most of us commute back and forth from our jobs. In outside sales, there is a "terrific" or "horrendous" amount of windshield time depending on your perspective. That is time we spend just sitting behind the wheel driving. The temptation is to use this to catch up on voicemail or phone calls. That's dangerous, so I have a hard time recommending it. If you do have a hands-free set, that may help, but doesn't eliminate all the danger.

I find driving to be a great time to think, plan, rehearse a call or presentation. I also use my automobile as a university or training center on wheels. I'm not a *Rhodes Scholar* but I am a *Roads Scholar*, constantly listening to recordings of educators, trainers and books while driving. I also keep all my *Apple* devices packed with inspirational music that helps keep me in a positive frame of mind. When the mind is not given direction, it can easily go negative.

Think about your time gaps. How can you fill those gaps with energizing strengths based activities that lead to your most authentic goals?

"By intentionally multi-purposing activities you can accomplish so much more than doing each activity individually."

~Shelly Flett

CHAPTER 35
Practice

Al couldn't find work in the area of his passion. He wanted to be a physics professor but apparently no one would hire him. No employer thought he was sufficiently qualified.

He took a job as a patent clerk. He could have said to himself, "I just don't have what it takes to work as a physics professor. I should give it up and find work in something else." But Al continued to work on the problems of physics during odd moments. He wrote the two most significant papers of his career while working in the clerks office.

After these two papers were published, there wasn't a university in the world that wouldn't have been proud to have Albert Einstein on their roster of physics professors.

One of my favorite stories is shared by *Peak Performance* author Charles Garfield. Garfield shares, "One day I was driving from my home in Northern California to the San Francisco airport, consumed with the talk I was flying to give. I found myself in early morning rush hour traffic, and then a real Manhattan-style traffic jam. I wasn't going anywhere. All of a sudden I hear loud rock music. I looked up and couldn't believe what I saw. The toll taker I was approaching was dancing!

I said, 'Please, Lord, not this morning. It's not a time for one of your tests.'

Anyway, I got to the toll booth and gave him my dollar. He gave me my change with a backhand slap, moving in time with his music. Now, I can't go through life pretending that these amazing things are not happening. So I asked the toll taker a standard, in depth research question, 'What are you doing?'

He said, 'I'm having a party.'

I said, 'What about the rest of these people?'

He said, 'They're not invited.'

I thought, 'This guy is either nuts, or he's going to teach me something.'

I couldn't find out then, but a month later I did. It was during the middle of the day, so there was no traffic, and he was still dancing, the music was still blaring. He insisted he was having a party. I told him that I studied high achievers for a living, and that I needed a certain kind of story.

He said, 'You want to study - great, take me to dinner.'

After dinner, I asked him what kept him going. I explained the concept of personal mission.

He said, 'You want to know my mission? I'm going to be a dancer someday. With what they pay me in that toll booth, I can't afford dance lessons. So I have the same two choices every other person has. I can let my dream die, or I can dance in the toll booth.' "

Garfield continues, "Now here is the key issue. There are 16 other people just like him, with the same job and no special privileges. They are members of what I call the 'complain and moan' school. These are the people who say, 'Oh, it's miserable. My boss won't let me do it. The organization won't let me do it. My parents didn't let me do it. The school system ruined me.' Yet one guy had managed to see a different world and a different set of possibilities. **He was saying to all of us, 'I can let my dream die, or I can make it work anyway.' "**

How can you combine your current work with tasks that make progress toward a job that fits you better, even your dream job? Some of my book *The STRENGTHSPATH Time Manager*, was loosely based on curriculum I had written for a corporate university syllabus. I practiced training and coaching while working with clients as a sales representative and then later in my role as a manager. Neither were my dream job, but I figured out methods to use my talents in ways that looked toward my career dreams. Just like rooms can be multi-purpose, so can tasks and activities.

In Einstein's case, there is some historical evidence that his supervisor at the patent office wasn't thrilled that he was using his clerking time to write papers on theoretical physics. There can be ethical issues involved with multi-purposing your activities. Always take the high road!

"Stripping away non-unique ability activities is the first step on this path. Michelangelo once said, 'As the marble wastes, the statue grows.' As the sculptor of your own life, you must chisel away all the extra marble that obscures who you really are."

~Catherine Nomura, Julia Waller, Shannon Waller

CHAPTER 36
Prune

In horticulture, you are probably aware that there is a process called pruning. It involves selectively removing parts of a plant like branches, buds or roots. The central purpose of pruning is to accelerate the health and growth of the plant or tree. Areas targeted for removal are diseased, damaged, decayed, dead or unproductive elements of the plant. Proper pruning increases the yield and quality of the flowers or fruit. Famously, Jesus Christ used this as a powerful metaphor explaining how to live a full productive life.

Dr. Robert Schuller, founder of the *Crystal Cathedral Congregation* in Garden Grove, California, is a hero of mine at so many levels. My Mom, Dad, both sets of Grandparents and myself tuned into his weekly *Hour of Power* broadcasts. I still have my Dad's copy of Dr. Schuller's early book, *Move Ahead With Possibility Thinking*. His teaching and ministry got me through some of the most difficult times of my life. In one of Schuller's later books, *If It Is To Be, It's Up To Me,* he writes on the concept of progressive early retirement, or what I call progressive pruning. As he moved through his career as a minister he systematically pruned away tasks that allowed him to be more productive.

Schuller begins, "How do I find the time to manage a weekly world-wide television ministry? And write books? And build a strong and happy family based on a loving marriage that's close to a joyous fiftieth anniversary?

I learned early in life how and when to 'retire'. I've now passed the forty-year anniversary in my ministerial work. At the end of my first year on the job as pastor I began to 'retire'. I retired from the job of janitor, for example. I haven't cleaned floors or toilets since! And that retirement freed up time for other duties. At the end of my second year I retired from my job as secretary, no longer typing my own letters. I found time to do other worthwhile church work. At the end of my third year, I retired as business manager. I haven't deposited money or written a check for the parish since then. I was released to use my time more productively. At the end of my fourth year, I retired as a department leader and teacher. I found the church a better replacement, and I had more time to write. At the end of my fifth year, then sixth year – yes, every passing year – I retired from further time consuming duties. At the end of my tenth year I finally retired as marriage counselor. The counseling center was opened and staffed as part of our ministry, and I found a lot of time – time that was instantly filled with new ideas that needed top priority on my clock and calendar. At the end of my fifteenth year we launched the television ministry, and I retired as the senior minister managing the staff of a large local congregation. At the end of my twenty-fifth year I retired as my car driver. I can now read books, dictate letters, and read my mail – all from the back seat of a car. At the end of my fortieth year I retired from five days a week in the office to become a minister at large in the world, filling a role only my face and name could fill."

Schuller continues, " Learn how to retire selectively from those duties you've always done. Focus on the role where you're irreplaceable. You'll be surprised at how well, wisely and fruitfully your time will then be managed." He exhorts us later in the book with some advice on what might inform our retirement choices when he says, "Look for something you enjoy and are pretty good at, and go for it."

When should you start this progressive pruning program? I think age eight works. The school system will object and you will still need to pitch in with family chores, but why not start early? Tiger Woods did and so did Warren Buffett.

From a strengths perspective, this means pruning away tasks and activities that aren't productive and don't enhance performance.

"I love creating partnerships; I love not having to bear the entire burden of the creative storytelling, and when I have unions like with George Lucas and Peter Jackson, it's really great; not only do I benefit, but the project is better for it."

~Steven Spielberg

CHAPTER 37
Partner

Tom Rath shares a story about the *Gallup* organization's economic development work in Puebla, Mexico. Found in his brilliant book, *Strengthsfinder 2.0,* the story offers a powerful example of what can happen when two people come together and contribute their innate abilities.

Hector was a world-class shoemaker, good enough to attract clients from all around the world. Yet he was continually frustrated with his business. He knew he was capable of crafting several hundred shoe pairs a week, but only averaged around thirty.

When asked why, Hector shared with a close friend how he was a poor salesman and equally ineffective collecting payments for his delivered orders. And he was forced to spend most of his time doing these activities that didn't come so naturally.

Now, if you are the average professional development trainer in America, you have a solution for Hector. You will get him in the classroom, offer coaching, or a set of "close the sale" recordings that will help Hector turn his weakness into a strength.

Fortunately for Hector, his friend was wiser than that. The friend introduced Hector to a naturally talented salesperson who could close sales as well as Hector could craft shoes. After only a year in the strengths-based partnership, this real world dynamic duo was producing, selling and collecting payments on three times more shoes. Hector had moved his business from 30 to over 100 pairs per week.

The best legal teams, and "Mad Men" advertising agencies have been benefiting from this Finder-Grinder-Minder Model for decades. The finder is the salesperson, the grinder produces the product or service and the minder takes care of the office along with the billing and such.

Many of us resist this because of constant exposure to messages suggesting that with enough grit and education we can do anything on our own. Certainly grit and education are critical components to any successful venture. But they become much more dynamic multipliers when combined with natural talent, both yours and your partners.

What's your innate talent? Are you a natural "Finder", "Grinder" or "Minder"?

History is also filled with terrific twosomes, dynamic duos, pairs of people who accomplish infinitely more together than they ever could have hoped to alone.

I for one, am a little bummed about the transition from Gotham Cities Dynamic Duo to the Dark Knight we see today. Don't get me wrong, I still love Batman. And he does team up with Alfred, Commissioner Gordon and others. But honestly, I miss Robin the Boy Wonder. What's the Lone Ranger without Tonto? What's the Cisco Kid without Poncho? What's Roy Rogers without Dale Evans?

Susy and I watched a *60 Minutes* segment on the creative team that has cranked out entertainment hits like *South Park*. I think Parker and Stone do cross the line and for that reason I'm not fond of what they create. But the creative process and teamwork they engage in is really fun to watch.

Teamwork really does make the dream work when that teamwork is solidly based on complimentary strengths. Mad Man Leo Burnett was the creative guy and Richard Heath was the sales guy in the famed advertising agency named after Burnett.

World class investor Warren Buffet is known as "Mr. Enthusiasm". His partner Charlie Munger has been dubbed the "No-Man" for his skeptical approach.

At *Disney*, Michael Eisner was the idea man and Frank Wells was the finance guy during one of that organization's most profitable runs. When Wells passed away in 1994, Eisner was never quite able to create the same brand of magic. He knew that too. Eisner has gone on to write a terrific book on productive partnerships titled *Working Together: Why Great Partnerships Succeed.*

Hewlett-Packard, the company we have come to know today as simply *HP*, was also formed on such a partnership between Bill Hewlett and Dave Packard. As with all the examples, their abilities tended to be complimentary. One was better at circuit technology while the other was better at manufacturing.

Bill Gates and Steve Ballmer had a similar partnership at *Microsoft*. Running the company isn't Gates' strong point and he knows that. Gates has a different kind of partnership with his wife Melinda in their philanthropic work.

Susy and I went to see the iconic Irish rock band *U2* in 20ll at the *Anaheim Stadium* in California. The *360 Tour* had just broken all attendance records for any band for all time. It was a terrific night. I have grown to love *U2's* music but I love what they stand for on the world's stage even more. Band leader Bono's work in behalf of the world's poor and disadvantaged is even more spectacular than his dazzling sets, on stage antics or smooth tenor voice.

One other spectacular thing about *U2* is their amazing longevity as a band. The band formed in 1976 and I'm writing in 2012. That's 36 years Bono, the Edge, Adam Clayton and Larry Mullen have been together.

How does this happen? I'm convinced it's because, as ego driven as lead singer Bono can be, at the end of the day he understands the limitations of his own talents and how much each band member contributes to the whole. In a lengthy biographical interview-turned-book with Michka Assayas, Bono shares his grasp of this, "I'm a lousy guitar player and an even lousier piano player. Had I not got Edge close by who was an extraordinarily gifted complex musician, I would be hopeless. Had I not got Larry and Adam, these melodies would not be grounded. But it's still very difficult for me to have to rely. Your weakness, the blessing of your weakness is it forces you into friendships."

Athletic teams, surgical teams, computer companies and rock bands can do great things together with an understanding of individual talents and complimentary roles.

Many people are doing what they are designed to do, but only partially. Maybe you are in a situation where half of what you do fits very well but the other half doesn't. There isn't always a solution to this. But sometimes you can negotiate a restructuring of your position with your company. Sometimes you can get it accomplished "off the books" by trading activities.

Some workers would be much more effective if they were doing a very focused subset of their current responsibilities. They need to specialize. An individualized version of what Jack Welch did with *General Electric* would be perfect.

When Welch took over *G.E.* in 1981, it was a respectable company. But it was a very diverse company that included 350 different businesses. Welch believed *G.E.* could be even better. What was his strategy? He used the *STRENGTHSPATH Principle*. He Discovered what *G.E.* was best at, Developed those businesses, and then Delivered them in a very focused way out in the marketplace.

In his own words, Welch describes the process, "To the hundreds of businesses and product lines that made up the company we applied a single criterion: can they be number 1 or number 2 at whatever they do in the world marketplace? Of the 348 businesses or product lines that could not, we closed some and divested others. Their sale brought in almost $10 billion. We invested $18 billion in the ones that remained and further strengthened them with $17 billion worth of acquisitions. What remained in 1989 were 14 world-class businesses, each one either first or second in the world market in which it participates."

Most workers could benefit from a personalized version of what *G.E.* did. Think about how you can close down some of the activities you aren't the best at. Sell off or outsource some others.

A few workers would be much more effective if they did just the opposite and expanded their duties. Some people are very gifted with broad categories of work and thrive on variety. They need to generalize.

Expanding

Generalize or increase variety. A few workers would be much more effective if they did just the opposite and expanded their duties. Some people are very gifted with broad categories of work and thrive on variety. They need to generalize.

Are you a brain surgeon that would be happier as a general practitioner? Some people are wired for variety. Doing the same thing day after day just doesn't work for them.

"Working on different types of projects can quickly widen your professional experience. You can quickly build the accomplishments section of your resume. If project teams are created and deconstructed on a project-by-project basis, you will have the opportunity to continually meet new people and expand your professional network."

~Eric Bloom

CHAPTER 38
Projects

Google offers its employees an opportunity to spend 20% of their time on side projects. *Gmail* was the very profitable result of one of those projects.

Facebook is also a company that encourages side projects and specifically encourage a strengths oriented approach. They allow employees to match their skills with points of interest and never force unnatural talent when linking team members to specific projects. Monthly strengths based "hackathons", usually all-night meetings, have turned out some of their most popular features including *Timeline*, *Chat* and *Video Messaging*.

Yankee Candles started as a side project. While at college, founder Michael J Kittredge decided to make candles at his parents' house as a side business while completing his education. When his parents decided they couldn't deal with having candles everywhere, Kittredge expanded. In 1998, he sold the company for more than $500 million.

Craig Newmark set up an email list so that he could keep up with his friends. The email list became unmanageable and Newmark moved it to a simple website. He worked at his day job for three more years before he cut the anchor to pursue *Craigslist* full time.

I recommend looking for side projects that really play to your strengths. In my case, I never passed on an opportunity to develop curriculum or do a training workshop.

When I look back over my career, the biggest leaps forward always came as a result of taking on a project, often unpaid or occasionally with a small stipend. Each of these projects offered up opportunities to contribute my top strengths and eventually led to career advancement. Sometimes that advancement came a year or two later. But it always came.

Occasionally I hear someone say, "I'm not taking on extra work I don't get paid for." This reminds me of Earl Nightingale's metaphor about people who stand in front of the stove saying, "Give me some heat and then I'll put some wood in you." Life doesn't work that way. In real life, you put the wood in first, light the kindling and then the heat comes out. An understanding of this simple principle would change so many lives.

The first place to take on strengths based projects is **inside your current organization**. If you're in a role that isn't offering opportunities to maximize your strengths, look for special projects that do. If there aren't any, create them. In some cases you may need permission, in others you can just start working on something that utilizes your passion and talent.

The second place to look, still **in your organization, is a corner or piece of an existing project**. Look for the piece that matches your innate talent and interest. Don't try to take over anyone else's role. Look for something that isn't getting done and dive in. Progressive organizations encourage this and in some cases set aside time for these side projects.

The third place to look is **in organizations that are outside the one where you earn a living**. Maybe it's a project in your church or community organization. Many of my best talents were first developed in volunteer roles. My primary strength activities are research, writing, training and coaching. These activities make me feel strong. Each of them was developed first in volunteer settings.

The fourth place to look is **independent project work**. This may mean starting a side business. Or it may mean doing the work you love as a hobby. I have a close friend who consistently made over one hundred thousand dollars each year taking on Saturday projects. His day job earned a similar amount of money combining for a very strong paycheck.

I recommend *The 10% Entrepreneur* by Patrick McGinnis and *The Leap* by Rick Smith. They outline low-risk ways of getting started.

When you take on an opportunity or create one, make sure your regular work doesn't suffer. Always stay focused on the primary contribution you're being paid for.

Finally, always make sure you do a fantastic job on the extra project. This will probably mean working a few nights and weekends. The combination of maintaining your regular work while adding extra value on a strengths based project should create opportunities for more strengths based projects.

Eventually, opportunities should occur to begin using those strengths as part of your regular job. If not, you will have built a resume that will allow you to take your talents where they are valued.

I have always been involved in work that is very project oriented with the banding and disbanding of work teams. I love this way of working.

Volunteer

Most of my research, writing, training and coaching skills were developed while working as an unpaid volunteer. I wrote curriculum and did training programs at churches. I also volunteered for a community crisis line. This was the beginning of my coaching career.

Offering up your natural talents and work activities that make you feel strong are one method of job shaping.

Offering up your strengths is referred to as your, "Come-To-Me-Whens"…. in Marcus Buckingham's *StandOut* training.

For example:

Come To Me When you have an editing project…

Come To Me When You have a carpentry project…

Come To Me When you need your computer fixed…

Your innate talent and passion, those activities that make you feel strong, are also the areas where your organization or business unit can rely on you for the biggest contributions. When properly directed, these strengths should allow you to add the most value to your team.

What are the situations where you want your colleagues to approach you for help? Where do you add the most value? What are the circumstances where you make the biggest contribution?

Write down potential "Come To Me When" tasks and activities. After putting together a good group of ideas, try to narrow the list down to three or four.

My Personal Examples:

Come To Me When… You need research, writing, training and coaching around strengths oriented career development.

Come To Me When… You need help with strengths oriented job crafting.

Come To Me When… You need help Discovering, Directing, Describing, Developing or Delivering your strengths in the marketplace.

When you put your list together, be as specific as you can. In my case, I love to write and create curriculum. This means I love to string together ideas, concepts, stories and steps of practical use on topics that interest me. I'm really only interested in writing on topics that relate to career development and helping people find work that fits them. I also hate editing and I'm terrible at it. Many writers are. I appreciate good design and layout but I'm not great at that either. I research and assemble content from other top experts and from my own experiences.

Ask your colleagues and those who report to you for their "Come To Me When…." list.

• Look for opportunities to collaborate and put together ad hoc teams.

• Create an informal marketing campaign to get the word out.

• Put together a spread sheet or a file system that profiles your team members' "Come To Me When" requests.

And **MAKE SURE** you provide opportunities for your colleagues and co-workers to do what they do best!

Volunteer opportunities often create direct professional opportunities, or as they did for me, offer opportunities to refine skills associated with my talent and passion. But as Christopher Penn suggests, volunteering your strengths also makes a bigger impact.

Penn writes in his blog, "When you look for volunteer opportunities, consider what you're good at. Ladling soup at a soup kitchen is important work, unquestionably, but if you're not good at working with people or food, perhaps it's not the biggest impact you can make."

Penn offers some terrific examples:

"Suppose you're a finance expert – could you instead volunteer to help families do their taxes, or help a non-profit straighten out its cash flow accounting issue?

Suppose you're a talented writer or copy editor – could you volunteer to help a non-profit write compelling donor copy or clean up its website?

Suppose you're an amazing chef – could you not only help prepare meals at a soup kitchen, but optimize the menu and budget to provide nutritious food while stretching limited dollars most effectively?"

Volunteering your strengths is a great career strategy, but it's also a great life strategy. Go volunteer for something!

"Every person requires particular conditions for his giftedness to thrive."

~Arthur F. Miller

CHAPTER 39
Place

I love snow globes, the kind you can shake up and create snow. They are miniature environments. It's a reminder that we're all designed to be positive environment creators. In fact, we create environments constantly whether we are aware of it or not. I love terrariums and ecospheres for the same reason.

Designer Michael Graves writes, "The objects that surround us are more than a measure of who we are, they also affect the way in which we live." To some extent, environmental design does shape our destiny.

Sharon Birkman writes, "You don't plant a ficus where a cactus is going to grow and then expect it to thrive." And Mike Murdock echoes, "Pineapples do well in Hawaii. They do not do well in Alaska. Atmosphere matters."

As I finish up this manuscript, Susy and I are housesitting for our son and daughter-in-law and taking care of Tina Fey and Dolly Parton, two French Bulldogs. I can't tell you the positive impact this environment has made on both my writing productivity and our collaborations in editing. Environment does matter!

But what are the malleable components of an environment? Here is a short list to get you started:

Positive Energy
Lighting

Color
A View
Privacy
Fresh Air
Scent
Silence
Music
Nature
Order
A Working Kitchen
A Library
Favorite Objects
Comfortable Furniture
Beauty
Art
Change

Deep Work and Eudaimonia Machines

Recently, there has been some criticism leveled at software development companies suggesting that the often used "open work" spaces do not provide an optimized environment for what Cal Newport and others call "deep work". This should be a consideration and a quiet, less interactive work space may be included in some cases.

In Newport's book *Deep Work* he writes, "We find ourselves in distracting open offices where inboxes cannot be neglected and meetings are incessant – a setting where colleagues would rather you respond quickly to their latest email than produce the best possible results." I know just what Newport is taking about. In my last corporate gig, offices were shuffled due to growth and I was placed in an office with my partner. We worked very well together, but not in the same office. I couldn't hear myself think. I had to negotiate for a change immediately. It meant I went on the road to satellite offices more frequently.

In *Deep Work*, Newport also talks about architecture professor David Dewane's *Eudaimonia Machine*. Eudaimonia is an ancient Greek word that can be translated as happiness or more accurately human flourishing. Dewane's concept is a brilliant design.

The first room in Dewane's set up is **The Gallery**. The purpose of The Gallery is to inspire and it contains examples or photographs of the organization's best work..

The second room is **The Salon**. This room is designed to a place to debate, think, even brood a bit. It is optimally furnished with great coffee, Wi-Fi and couches.

The Library is the third room. It includes work relevant books, magazines and other resources including copiers and scanners designed to collect project information.

The fourth room is **The Office**. Designed for collaboration, this room has a conference table, but also cubicles with desks. It would have a whiteboard and perhaps a projection system for presentations.

The final and fifth room of the Eudaimonia Machine is **The Chamber** or **Deep Work Chambers**. Actually a set of chambers, this area contains multiple 6x9 rooms protected by thick soundproofing material. The purpose of these chambers is to provide space for complete focus and uninterrupted work.

The Eudaimonia Machine may sound a bit utopian, but is it really? Is it really that much more far-fetched than separate kitchens, bathrooms, bedrooms and such? Maybe in your current situation you need to travel around to use your different rooms. Think about your local library and the neighborhood *Starbucks*. Think about the different types of work you perform. How can you shape the environments? How can you optimize the atmosphere?

Olan Mills' "Double Office"

I worked for 16 years in the *Olan Mills* organization and had the opportunity of visiting Mr. Mills' office. He kept two offices. The outer office was opulent, immaculate and designed for meetings and receiving guests. On one occasion, I got inside his working office. Chaos! Books and papers everywhere. When I subsequently purchased my first new house, I remembered and arranged a similar set up. It was a brilliant solution. In the outer office, I could look smart by all the cultural standards and then work effectively in my inner sanctum.

Tom Peters has written many incredibly helpful business books. One was titled, *Thriving On Chaos.* People in some positions do just that. Dee Hock, the founder of *Visa*, coined a word that immediately resonated with me..."Chaordic". It's the blend of chaos and order.

Albert Einstein sported one of the messiest work environments one could imagine and yet he was one of the best thinkers in history. In their book *A Perfect Mess*, Eric Abrahamson and David H. Freedman argue that a messy desk can be an attribute of an effective worker. They offer compelling research along with many examples other than Einstein.

I'm not trying to make a case for working in a mess. My point is that the whole matter is an issue of individual strengths. Some people work more effectively from chaos, some a chaordic blend and others from perfect order. I would also add that cutting edge science suggests that what looks like chaos on the surface is very ordered underneath.

The *Zappos* Trip

Susy and I went to Las Vegas for our third anniversary in 2011. We went to an amazing Celine Dion concert, ate at *Bobby Flay's Mesa Grill* and stopped by *The Bald Man - Max Brenner's* for chocolate milkshakes.

Another highlight was the trip and tour at *Zappos*, the online shoe retail company. *Zappos* is known for its stellar customer service and return policies. I believe their secret is creating a fun work environment. Personal workspace decorations are all fun, with some bordering on outrageous. They all reflect the unique individual interests of each team member. Make sure your workspace reflects your passion, talent and values.

Agile Scrum's War Room

Agile Scrum often refers to the work space as the **War Room**. It is optimally designed in a way that all team members can move freely, communicate and get their work done.

Sprint author and *Google Ventures* designer Jake Knapp talks about the value of a great War Room set up on a blog post titled, *Why your team needs a war room and how to set one up.* Jake, who has worked on over 80 start up teams says, "I've learned that a dedicated work space with walls – a war room – always helps us do better work. The walls of a war room can extend a team's memory, provide a canvas for shared note-taking, and act as long-term storage for works in progress."

Jake continues, "In a *Google Ventures* design sprint, it's common to have many things on the walls at once: user story diagrams, research notes, printouts of existing user interface, sketches of possible solutions, a detailed storyboard, and sometimes more." Knapp recommends a dedicated project room, as many whiteboards as you can fit and flexible furniture.

Maybe you can't swing your own Eudaimonia Machine just yet. I get it. I'm not there either, but I do have a vision for it. Start with a plant in your office and a nice scent for your car. Then build on it.

Geography

Location… Location… Location… is the mantra of retail. There is a strengths based geography of success that involves signature locations and job shaping. One I call the "Nashville Principle" or "Taylor Swift Strategy". As a teenager, Taylor Swift decided she wanted to be a music star. She talked her parents into moving the whole family to Nashville. Taylor had decided her path went through Nashville and her parents agreed. Sometimes you can't get to your signature destination from where you are. You'll have to move.

Leadership expert, John Maxwell made a similar decision. He lived in San Diego with a near-paradise climate. But he looked at his strengths oriented signature direction of delivering keynote speeches every week. He looked at where most of the signature target organizations were located and he moved his whole company to Atlanta, Georgia. He freed up hours on his schedule that allowed him to crank out books and have more time with his wife Margaret.

In his book, *It's Your Time*, Joel Osteen shares the story about his friend Reuben who owned a struggling auto repair shop. One day Reuben spotted a "For Lease" sign on a nearby building that had great freeway exposure. He inspected the place, prayed for God's guidance and made the move. Within a short period of time, his business increased ten times!

Susy and I decided we wanted to live on California's Central Coast but we had no idea how to make the move happen. She was taking asthma medication and I had sinus problems requiring daily doses of *Advil* and decongestants. I had no income source there, we thought housing was too expensive and my parents, who are getting older, needed to live close by. I found a job as a career service coordinator. Then, further research revealed that Central Coast housing costs were similar when lower gas and electric bills were factored in. And finally, my parents agreed to relocate shortly after we did. When you get clear on what you want, God can open doors.

Where were you born to live? When I was a teenager, my optometrist suggested that I was born to live in Scotland because I have light sensitive eyes. Sunglasses are a must in my case. Susy wilts in the heat. The California's Central Coast is awesome on both counts.

Maybe you have a nomadic streak and were born for multiple locations. Susy and I traveled together for a year while I worked from a mobile office. It was great fun. There are bi-coastal couples who love this lifestyle.

Maybe you just need to move across town reducing your commute. I'm writing this section from Los Angeles where the commutes are horrendous. The 405 Freeway is affectionately called the parking lot. Some commuters could free up two to four hours a day by moving closer to their work.

Your refusal to relocate may also cost you job opportunities. Our daughter-in-law is a make-up artist for print advertising. Los Angeles is where the opportunity is for that type of work.

I recently spoke with a Sacramento dentist who refuses to hire an office worker, assistant or hygienist that lives across that city. He says they never stick with the job. The traffic just beats them up. I think you might be surprised how many employers know this.

If you want to be a dancer, Las Vegas or New York are your places. If you want to work in film, Hollywood is your place. If you want to work in animation, it is Los Angeles, Vancouver and London. Silicon Valley offers more technology opportunities as do Seattle and Austin. Most professions have hot spots that offer more and better opportunities.

There is a lot of research that suggests that genius clusters. There is more research suggesting that both happiness and unhappiness cluster. Health and longevity seem to cluster as well. Attitudes cluster. In an earlier chapter I shared the Jim Rohn quote, "You are the average of the five people you spend the most time with." This seems to be true at both the macro level dealing with larger areas and sections of a country. But it also seems to be true at the micro level involving communities, neighborhoods, friends and families.

Finding your tribe will always be a key component of success. This will always be somewhat related to geography. The internet has erased this a bit but not entirely.

Your dream job almost always comes with a specific location. Think about this as you select, re-select and shape your career into one that fits.

"Switching from one career to another can be scary, but it also can be a thrilling experience. Look at it as an opportunity to really go after what you want to accomplish in life and make a difference in the world. The key is to take small, conscious steps and prepare yourself for a successful transition."

~Jack Canfield

CHAPTER 40
Position

Sometimes, in order to maximize your potential, you'll have to shift positions. Have you heard of Babe Ruth? Unless you're a baseball fan maybe not. If you have heard of him, you may know he's considered by some to be the best baseball hitter of all time. But unless you are among the most dedicated of baseball fans, you may not know that he started his professional career as a pitcher. He was a very good pitcher too. But at one point in his professional career, he made the decision to stop pitching so he could focus on a role where he was even better. **He was even heavily criticized for the decision**. Looking back, it was a pretty good choice. His decision to set aside the role of pitcher, where he was merely good, in favor of a role where he could become the world's greatest hitter, was life changing for him and his teammates.

Often the difference between being good and being great is making adjustments that allow you to spend more of your time developing your greatest strengths.

Do you need to use the "Babe Ruth" strategy? Do you need to figure out how to let go of tasks and activities where you don't have the potential to become the best? Maybe you need to be in another position all together. Or maybe you need to expand or reduce from a current role.

Strengths Strategist Marcus Buckingham estimates that as many as 80% of U.S. workers are in a role or position that needs adjustment if they are to maximize their performance and contribution in the workplace. About 1/3 of that 80% are **playing the wrong position all together.** A second 1/3 would perform much better if they were **working in a pared down or more focused version of their current role.** And a final 1/3 would actually contribute more if they worked in a **more expanded version of their current role.**

What about you?

Often the difference between being good and being great is making adjustments that allow you to spend more of your time delivering your greatest strengths.

Ever had an annual performance review where the focus quickly shifted to a discussion about how to fix your weaknesses? It's an all-too-common scenario. And it's probably a waste of time. It's a much better idea to build on your strengths.

Do you want to go from good to great? Focus on your natural talents and passions. Why? Because you will develop faster and better, doing what you do best and enjoy most. These are your strengths and they are yours for life.

You can build on them, and they won't let you down. Think about it: What would your life be like if you got paid to do what you do best and truly enjoy? Awesome, isn't it?

Transitions and Transfers

In an earlier chapter I mentioned Steve Harvey's book, *Think Like A Success, Act Like A Success.* Steve shares this idea of a bus transfer, "Think about this in terms of traveling on a city bus from one location to the next. Often you have to get a transfer in order to complete the journey. You will then be led to another transfer, which will take you to your second vehicle." The same analogy works if you are more familiar with air travel. We all want non-stop destination flights sitting in first class with someone bringing us drinks. But none of us start there.

Harvey then moves on to tell about his own career transfers. He worked very hard physical jobs until he was inspired by an old friend (Arsenio Hall) to take his shot at comedy at age 30.

Consider his career path and the transfers:

Amateur Night – Working for Free

Paid Gigs - $25.00 a Night

Featuring Act - $350.00 per Week

Featuring Act II - $750.00 per Week

Small Club National Headliner - $1500.00 per Week

Large Club National Headliner - $60,000 per Week

Large Club - $25,000 per Night

Consider that in order to go forward, you may have to go backward for a short period. Notice that Steve Harvey started out working for free and then for a non-livable wage. You may have to take an unpaid internship and work for minimum wage for a few months before you begin your climb.

Harvey asks a great question, "Are you so busy looking for the luxury vehicle now, that your level of development can't afford it?"

People who are successful have big dreams but they are willing to start very small. Identify a big target or dream job and then backward map it. And it's okay to change dreams as you get closer. Sometimes dreams look different up close. But get started!

"Just a spoon full of sugar helps the medicine go down."
~Mary Poppins

Chapter 41
Poppins

Sometimes you just have to suck it up and get it done. That doesn't mean it has to be a completely horrible experience. *Mary Poppins* was written at *Walt Disney* studios in tandem with five other films. It was the greatest live action success of Walt's career. It won five *Oscars* including *Best Song* and *Best Music, Original Score*. *Disney* song writers Richard and Robert Sherman offered some insight on how one of the most popular Poppins' songs came about.

One of the early songs got rejected and that rejection came with a request for a "quick-smart" more Mary Poppins-like tune. One of the Sherman brothers was at home that night talking to his young son about the vaccination he'd received at school that day. Sherman asked, "Did it hurt?" "No", the son replied, "They dropped the medicine onto a sugar cube. It was a piece of cake."

The next day the idea was shared back at the studio, "What do you think of, 'A spoon full of sugar helps the medicine go down?' " As the brothers played with the idea, they came up with another hallmark of the tune... "When Mary sang 'down' in the song, the music mood should go up."

And so it was, Mary Poppins offered up one of the last solutions we all need on occasion. She sang the answer, "Just A Spoon Full Of Sugar, Helps The Medicine Go Down… In The Most Delightful Way."

When my wife chops vegetables, she turns on the *Home and Garden Channel*. A few sessions of *Flip or Flop*, *The Property Brothers* and *Fixer Upper* makes the chopping go by faster.

A lot of people slap on the headphones… If you have to get it done… Try combining what you love with what you hate.

I worked for many years in outside selling. Cold calling was the part of my work that I enjoyed the least. I had a particular distaste for telephone cold calling and appointment setting. On appointment setting days I would set a cookie up in front of me or some other sweet thing and after each call I'd break off a small corner and treat myself.

I've always liked exercise and have been able to find methods that were enjoyable. Some people struggle with this and need to implement the Poppins Solution. For some that's music. There's actually research suggesting that upbeat music makes exercise easier for everyone. Others do much better in a group exercise environment like a class. Some combine with dance like *Zumba*. And others find that a personal coach is the ticket.

As I've gotten older, most of my walks are now on the beach with Susy. I combine my yoga style stretching with a hot shower. As of this writing, I'm adding back in some high intensity sprinting to our beach walks along with some some body weight strength training like pushups and squats.

At work, I believe that most people should strive for a job that is at minimum 80% enjoyable. That 80% should be so enjoyable that you can't wait to get out of bed and get there. Many of us can move well past that 80%. That may require some serious job shaping or even a career change but it is attainable.

But most of us will have a handful of things each week that we find less enjoyable. As it turned out, *Disney* himself faced some tough medicine while trying to get the film made. The movie was based on *Mary Poppins*, the book, written by the prickly author P.L. Travers. The author came on the set and tried to sabotage the film because she disliked Disney's sentimental version. Tom Hanks and Emma Thompson brilliantly portray the difficulty in the recent film, *Saving Mr. Banks*.

Try the Mary Poppins technique. If you need some inspiration, save the clip and replay as needed: https://youtu.be/HrnoR9cBP3o

Mary Poppins (Julie Andrews) begins:
"In every job that must be done…
There is an element of fun…
You find the fun and snap…
The jobs a game…
And every task you take…
Becomes a piece of cake!"

What's your spoon full of sugar?

"At its root, Scrum is based on a simple idea: whenever you start a project, why not regularly check in, see if what you're doing is heading in the right direction. And question whether there are any ways to improve how you're doing what you're doing, any ways of doing it better and faster, and what might be keeping you from doing that."

~Jeff Sutherland

CHAPTER 42
Plan

"Write the vision and make it plain on tablets, that he may run who reads it."
~Habakkuk 2:2

Your strengths won't get used unless you plan for it. You must intentionally set aside the time. Vacations rarely happen unless you put them on the calendar and arrange for time off.

Great managers use scoreboards and dashboards to keep everyone aware of progress. Carl Pearson was the father of modern business statistics and is known for Pearson's Law: "When performance is measured, performance improves." And the corollary: "When performance is measured and reported, it improves exponentially." This is true even at the international economic level. The countries that measure and quantify have the strongest thriving economies.

In *Agile Planning*, the project to-do list (called a Back-Log List) goes on a "Do" - "Doing" - "Done" board that is often referred to by the Japanese name Kanban (meaning "Card You Can See"). In the Scrum framework, it goes by ScrumBoard.

I like the "Do" – "Doing" – "Done" format because it perfectly matches the **Y.E.S.** time frames I use in passion assessment. Is there a **Yearning** before you begin the items on the "Do" list? Is there **Engagement** with a growing sense of energy and timelessness while you're "Doing" the items?

Is there a sense of **Satisfaction** after you've "Done" the items on the list? The Kanban Board can provide a terrific strengths check-in.

You can easily build your own Kanban on a sheet of paper, poster board, grease board or using an online tool. If you go with the online option, I recommend *Trello.com* which is what I use. It's easy to learn and can be reconfigured and shared easily.

The format below is a Kanban set up for personal strengths use, execution and implementation:

Potential – This is a place to brainstorm possible strengths.

Planned – Make notes on strengths use planning.

Progress – Make note of activities and tasks accomplished.

Pattern – When a routine is scheduled and adhered to make a note in this column.

POTENTIAL	PLANNED	PROGRESS	PATTERN
Writing	Books Blog Posts Articles	Blog Set Up	Writing 30 Minutes Daily
Speaking	YouTube Workshops Seminars Keynotes	5 YouTubes	Writing YouTube Scripts

Strength Activation Sprints

A Sprint is a time-boxed process of one month or less, where an individual or team implements a set of Tasks. A common Sprint length is 21 days but it can be up to 30 days or as little as one week. If you're just introducing the concept, you can shorten your Sprint length to a single day or even an hour or less for a walk-through or training purposes.

You can also combine it with the *Pomodoro* concept to work with 25 minute increments.

The idea of a Sprint is to completely finish an increment of a project. A Strength Sprint could be intentionally using any strength for 21 days. A Strength Sprint is all about intentionally executing a top strength for a pre-determined time frame.

Bibliography

Read This First!

Peter Buffett, *Life Is What You Make It: Find Your Own Path To Fulfillment* (New York: Harmony Books, 2010).

Prologue

M. Night Shyamalan, *Unbreakable* (Touchstone Pictures, 2002).

Richard Chang, *The Passion Plan: A Step-by-Step Guide to Discovering, Developing and Living Your Passion* (New York, Jossey Bass, 2000).

Bill Burnett & Dave Evans, *Designing Your Life: How to Build a Well-Lived Joyful Life* (New York: Knopf, 2016).

Marcus Buckingham and Don O. Clifton, *Now, Discover Your Strengths* (New York: Free Press/Simon & Schuster, 2001).

Nicholas Lore, *The Pathfinder: How to Choose or Change Your Career for a Lifetime of Success and Satisfaction* (New York: Touchstone/Simon & Schuster, 2011), 12-13.

Portia Nelson, *Autobiography – 5 Chapters, Becoming Who You Are*, http://www.becomingwhoyouare.net/autobiography-in-5-short-chapters-by-portia-nelson/ .

Section I - The Cultural Problem

Chapter 1 Deception: Default Paths

Bob McDonald and Don E. Hutcheson, *Don't Waste Your Talent* (Marietta, Georgia: Longstreet Press, 2000), xi.

Seth Godin, *Default Settings Rule The World*, https://www.propublica.org/article/set-it-and-forget-it-how-default-settings-rule-the-world.

Tony Gaskins, *Dream Chaser: If You Don't Build Your Dream Someone Will Hire You To Build Theirs* (Hoboken: John Wiley, 2017) .

Chapter 2 Deception: Hot Jobs

Chapter 3 Deception: Dead End Jobs

Susan Steele, *From Grills Heat to Power Suite*, https://www.questia.com/newspaper/1P2-33006136/from-grill-s-heat-to-mcdonald-s-power-suite-susan .

Marcus Buckingham, *The One Thing You Need to Know* (New York: Free Press/Simon & Schuster, 2005), 250-253.

Patrick McCarthy with Robert Spector, *The Nordstrom Way* (New York: John Wiley, 1995) .

Matthew B. Crawford, *Shop Class As Soulcraft: An Inquiry Into The Value Of Work* (New York: Penguin, 2009).

Chapter 4 Deception: You Can't Make Money At That

Nathan Gebhard, Brian McAllister and Mike Marriner with Jay Sacher, Alyssa Frank, Annie Mais, Jaime Zehler and Willie Witte, *Roadmap: The Get-It-Together Guide for Figuring Out What To Do with Your Life* (San Francisco: Chronicle Books, San Francisco, 2015), 156-157.

Thomas J. Stanley, *The Millionaire Mind* (Kansas City: Andrews McMeel, 2001).

Chapter 5 Deception: Degreeism

https://www.consumerreports.org/student-loan-debt-crisis/lives-on-hold/ .

http://www.rateitall.com/t-20542-success-without-a-college-degree.aspx.

Chapter 6 Deception: Job Description Confusion

O*NET (The Occupational Information Network), https://www.onetonline.org/link/summary/13-2011.01.

Chapter 7 Deception: Parental Advice

Jack and Suzy Welch, *Winning: The Ultimate Business How To Book* (New York: Harper Collins, 2005), 265-266.

Byron Reeves and J. Leighton Reid, *Total Engagement: Using Games and Virtual Worlds to Change the Way People Work and Businesses Compete* (Boston: Harvard Business School Publishing, 2009).

Chapter 8 Deception: You Can't Do Anything

Hoda Kotb, *Where We Belong: Journeys That Show Us The Way* (New York: Simon & Schuster, 2016), 1-49.

Ben Carson, *You Have A Brain: A Teen's Guide To Thinking Big,* (Grand Rapids: Zondervan, 2015), 90-93.

Melinda Doolittle, *"I'm Tone Deaf",* Chicken Soup for the American Idol Soul (Deerfield Beach: Health Communications, 2007).

Chapter 9 Deception: You Can Do Anything

Jennifer Fox, *Your Child's Strengths* (New York: Viking, 2008).

https://www.businessinsider.com/anders-ericsson-how-to-become-an-expert-at-anything-2016-6 .

Chapter 10 Deception: Anyone Can Do This

Bobb Biehl, *Focusing Your Life* (Masterplanning: 2001).

Marcus Buckingham and Don Clifton, *Now, Discover Your Strengths* (New York: Free Press, 2001)

Johari Window Explanation, https://en.wikipedia.org/wiki/Johari_window.

Chapter 11 Deception: Change Your Personality

Chapter 12 Deception: Deficit Attention Disorder

Don O. Clifton and Paula Nelson, *Soar With Your Strengths* (New York: Dell Publishing, 1992).

George Reavis, *Animal School Parable*, https://www.forbes.com/sites/georgebradt/2011/12/07/lessons-from-the-animal-school-fable-in-leveraging-strengths/#5976b80a3ea4.

John Maxwell, *Talent Is Never Enough* (Nashville: Thomas Nelson, 2007).

Chapter 13 Deception: Do Whatever It Takes

Chapter 14 Deception: Work On Your Weakness

Jay Niblick, *What's Your Genius?* (James Publishing, 2009).

Steve Roesler, *Does Focusing on Strengths Give An Excuse For Ignoring Weakness?*, https://www.allthingsworkplace.com/2007/04/when_strengths_.html.

Chapter 15 Deception: Divisions and Definitions

John B. Carroll, *Human Cognitive Abilities* (New York: Cambridge University Press, 1993).

Enneagram Institute, https://www.enneagraminstitute.com

Marcus Buckingham, *Go Put Your Strengths To Work* (New York: Free Press, 2007).

Howard Gardner, *Multiple Intelligence Theory Criteria*, https://www.intelltheory.com/mitheory.shtml.

Richard Bolles/Gary Bolles, *What Color Is Your Parachute?* (New York: Penguin/Random, 2017).

Chapter 16 Deception: Dichotomies – Work/Play

Dr. Wayne Dyer, *The Sky's The Limit* (New York: Pocket 1980), 112-114.

Charlie Gilke, *On Productive Play*, https://www.productiveflourishing.com/productive-play-the-middle-ground-between-work-and-play/.

244

Angela Duckworth, *Grit: The Power of Passion and Perseverance* (New York: Scribner/Simon & Schuster, 2016), 106.

Section II   Circumstances

Chapter 17 Dips – Dead Ends – Dead Horses

Seth Godin, *The Dip* (New York: Penguin/Portfolio, 2007).

Chapter 18 Disguises

The Buddha in Bangkok Story - Dr. Myles Munroe, *The Principles And The Power Of Vision* (New Kensington, Whitaker House, 2003),15.

The Gillian Lynne Story - Ken Robinson, *The Element* (New York: Penguin, 2009), 1-3.

Chapter 19 Dormancy and Delays

Ken Robinson, *The Element* (New York: Penguin, 2009), 258.

Arthur Miller, *Why You Can't Be Anything You Want To Be* (Grand Rapids: Zondervan, 1999).

David Epstein, *The Sports Gene – Inside The Science Of Extraordinary Athletic Performance* (New York: Penguin Group, 2014), 128-130.

Chapter 20 Dynamic Tension

Timothy Butler, *Getting Unstuck: A Guide To Discovering Your Next Career Path* (Boston: Harvard Press, 2010).

Chapter 21 Disempowering Forces

Timothy Butler, *Getting Unstuck: A Guide To Discovering Your Next Career Path* (Boston: Harvard Press, 2010), 31-35.

Richard Carson, *Taming Your Gremlin* (New York: Harper Collins, 2003).

Lance Wallnau, *Doing Business Supernaturally,* https://lancewallnau.com/doing-business-supernaturally/.

Joyce Meyer, *Battlefield of the Mind* (New York: Warner Faith, 1995).

Section III   The Strengthspath Solution

Chapter 22   Passion

Timothy Butler, *Getting Unstuck: A Guide To Discovering Your Next Career Path* (Boston: Harvard Press, 2010).

Oprah Winfrey, *The Best of Oprah's What I Know For Sure* (New York: The Oprah Magazine, Hearst Corporation, 2000), 39.

Chapter 23   Potential

Don O. Clifton and Paula Nelson, *Soar With Your Strengths* (New York: Dell Publishing, 1992).

Marcus Buckingham and Don O. Clifton, *Now, Discover Your Strengths* (New York: Free Press/Simon & Schuster, 2001).

Scott Adams-Creator, *"The Knack"* from *Dilbert: The Complete Series* (DVD) (Culver City: Sony Pictures, 2000), Season 1-Episode 9.

Howard Gardner, *Multiple Intelligences* (New York: Basic Books, New York, 1993), 17-26.

Margaret E. Broadley, *Your Natural Gifts* (McLean, Virginia: EPM Publications, 1977), 3-7.

O*NET (The Occupational Information Network), https://www.onetonline.org/find/descriptor/browse/Abilities/.

Tom Rath, *Strengthsfinder 2.0* (New York: Gallup Press, 2007).

Chapter 24   Personality

Tony Alessandra, Ph.D. and Michael J. O'Connor, Ph.D., *The Platinum Rule: Discover The Four Basic Business Personalities and How They Can Lead You To Success* (New York: Time Warner, 1996).

John Trent and Rodney Cox, *Leading From Your Strengths* (Nashville: B & H Publishing Group, 2004).

Jason Hedge, *The Essential DISC Training Workbook* (Redding: DISC-U, 2013).

Robert A. Rohm, Ph.D., *Positive Personality Profiles* (Atlanta: Personality Insights, 1992).

Isabel Briggs-Myers with Peter Myers, *Gifts Differing* (Mountain View: Davies-Black, 1995).

The Official MBTI® Manual (Sunnyvale: The Myers-Briggs Company).

Dario Nardi, Ph.D., *Neuroscience of Personality* (Los Angeles: Radiance House, 2011).

246

David Keirsey, *Please Understand Me II: Temperament, Character, Intelligence* (Del Mar: Prometheus Nemesis Book Company, 1998).

Chapter 25   Probe

Timothy Butler and James Waldroop, *Discovering Your Career in Business* (Reading: Perseus Books, 1997).

Arthur Miller, *Why You Can't Be Anything You Want To Be* (Grand Rapids: Zondervan, 1999).

Peter Drucker, *Managing Oneself* (Boston: Harvard Business Review, 2008).

Jay Niblick, *What's Your Genius?* (James Publishing, 2009).

Frank Parsons, *Choosing a Vocation* (New York: Houghton Mifflin, 1909).

Steve de Shazer and Insoo Kim Berg, *The Miracle Question* https://solutionfocused.net/what-is-solution-focused-therapy/

Jack Canfield, *The Success Principles* (New York: William Morrow/Harper Collins, 2005), 270-271.

Chapter 26   Polish

Anders Ericsson with Robert Pool, *Peak: Secrets from the New Science of Expertise* (New York: Houghton Mifflin, 2016).

Maxwell Maltz, *Psycho Cybernetics* (New York: Pocket Books, 1960).

Chapter 27   Package

Joshua Bell, *Subway Station Story*, https://www.thoughtco.com/a-violinist-in-the-metro-3299658.

Chapter 28   Promote

Chapter 29   Perform

Chapter 30   Persevere

Chapter 31   Parts

Anne Linden with Kathrin Perutz, *Mindworks* (Kansas City: Andrews McMeel, 1997), 205.

Ray Dalio, *Principles* (New York: Simon & Schuster, 2017), 157-162.

Marshall Goldsmith with Mark Reiter, *Triggers* (New York: Crown Business, 2015),140-151.

Chapter 32   Pace

Richard "Mack" Machowicz, *Unleash The Warrior Within* (New York: Marlowe and Company, 2002).

Chapter 33   Prime Time

Michael Breus, *The Power of When* (New York: Little Brown and Company, 2016).

Chapter 34   Plant

J.K. Rowling Biography, https://harrypotter.bloomsbury.com/uk/jk-rowling-biography/ .

Chapter 35   Practice

Charles Garfield, *Peak Performance – The New Heroes of American Business* (New York: Avon, 1986), 276-278.

Walter Isaacson, *Einstein – His Life and Universe* (New York: Simon & Schuster, 2007).

Chapter 36   Prune

Robert Schuller, *If It's Going To Be It's Up To Me* (San Francisco: Harper), 138.

Chapter 37   Partner

Michka Assayas, *Bono – In Conversation with Michka Assayas* (New York: Penguin Books, 2005).

Tom Rath, *Strengthsfinder 2.0* (New York: Gallup Press, 2007).

Michael Eisner, *Working Together: Why Great Partnerships Succeed* (New York: Harper Business, 2010).

Chapter 38   Projects

Eric Schmidt and Jonathan Rosenberg with Alan Eagle, *How Google Works* (New York: Grand Central Publishing, 2014).

Blake Beus, *Strengths-Based Approach to Better Productivity and Workplace Culture*, http://switchandshift.com/strengths-based-approach-culture .

Patrick McGinnis, *The 10% Entrepreneur* (New York: Portfolio/Penguin/Random House, 2016).

Rick Smith, *The Leap* (New York: Portfolio/Penguin/Random House, 2009).

Chapter 39   Place

Cal Newport, *Deep Work – Rules for Focused Success in a Distracted World* (New York: Grand Central Publishing, 2016).

How Cal Newport's Deep Work Will Influence Modern Office Design (Strong Project Modern Office Furniture, January 28, 2016), https://blog.strongproject.com/how-cal-newports-deep-work-concept-will-influence-office-design/ .

Eric Abrahamson and David H. Freedman, *A Perfect Mess* (New York: Back Bay/Little Brown & Company, 2007).

Tom Peters, *Thriving On Chaos – A Handbook for a Management Revolution* (New York: Alfred Knopf, 1987).

Dee Hock, *Birth of the Chaordic Age* (San Francisco: Berrett-Koehler Publishers,1999).

Taylor Swift Biography, https://www.biography.com/people/taylor-swift-369608 .

Eric Weiner, *The Geography of Genius* (New York: Simon & Schuster, 2016).

Jake Knapp, *Why Your Team Needs a War Room and How to Set One Up,* https://library.gv.com/why-your-team-needs-a-war-room-and-how-to-set-one-up-498e940e3487 .

Chapter 40   Position

Steve Harvey, *Act Like A Success Think Like A Success* (New York: Amistad/Harper Collins, 2014), 77-80.

Chapter 41   Poppins

Robert B. Sherman and Richard M. Sherman, *Spoon Full of Sugar*, from *Mary Poppins* (Burbank: Walt Disney Studios, 1964).

Chapter 42   Plan

"Write the vision and make it plain on tablets, that he may run who reads it." This passage from Habakkuk 2:2 is taken from the New King James Version published by Thomas Nelson.

Tycho Press, *Scrum Basics: A Very Quick Guide to Agile Project Management* (Berkeley: Tycho Press, 2015).

Jeff Sutherland, *Scrum: The Art of Doing Twice the Work in Half the Time* (New York: Crown Business, 2014).

Tridibesh Satpathy-Lead Author, *Scrum Study: A Guide to the Scrum Body of Knowledge* (Phoenix: Scrumstudy, 2013).

Jim Benson, Tonianne DeMaria Barry, *Personal Kanban: Mapping Work | Navigating Life* (Seattle: Modus Operandi Press, 2009).

Daniel Markovitz, *A Factory of One: Applying Lean Principles to Banish Waste and Improve Personal Performance* (Boca Raton: CRC Press, 2012).

Also by Dale Cobb

The STRENGTHSPATH Principle: Your Roadmap to Career Success

The STRENGTHSPATH Time Manager

Dream Job!!! A Strengths Based Guide To Job Search

Take This Job and Shape It

Strengths Oriented Selection

Look for these coming titles in the SUCCESSPATH Series:

The STRENGTHSPATH Guide to Selection and Hiring

The SUCCESSPATH Strategies: A Guide To Universal Success Principles

The STRENGTHSPATH Strategies: Succeeding by Doing What You Do Best

Crazy Good: A STRENGTHSPATH Guide to Discovering Your Natural Talents

Insanely Great: A STRENGTHSPATH Guide to Developing Your Talents Into Strengths

Wildly Successful: A STRENGTHSPATH Guide to Delivering Your Strengths in the Workplace

The STRENGTHSPATH Manager & Leader

The STRENGTHSPATH Sales Person

The STRENGTHSPATH Parent

Maximize Your Ministry: A STRENGTHSPATH Guide to Doing What You Do Best

The STRENGTHSPATH Educator

The Daily STRENGTHSPATH

SUCCESSPATH Sprint Coaching

One-to-One Sprints ☆ **60-Minute Seminars** ☆ **Workshops**
Modeling Projects ☆ **Performance Research**
Strengths Assessments ☆ **Selection** ☆ **Outplacement**

Strengths Oriented Career Development Sprints
Arrive! - Strengths Oriented Goal Sprints
Strengths Oriented Time Management Sprints
"A-Game" Sprints
Service Oriented Selling Sprints
Storyboarding – Customer Experience Journey Sprints

Connect Online

Follow Our SUCCESSPATH Sixty Second Seminars

LinkedIn https://www.linkedin.com/in/dalecobb

Facebook
https://www.facebook.com/successpathcareerdevelopment/

Twitter https://twitter.com/strengthspath

Website http://www.successpathcareerdevelopment.com

Vimeo https://vimeo.com/dalecobb

YouTube https://www.youtube.com/user/daleacobb

Tumblr https://www.tumblr.com/blog/dalecobb

Contact

Dale Cobb
P.O. Box 870
Grover Beach, CA 93483
805.668.9600